The Bible:
Reasons to Believe
It's God's Word

Daniel Mann

The Bible

Daniel Mann, Author
Tom Riley, Editor

The Bible:
Reasons to Believe It's God's Word

A Word of Thanks

The publication of this book would not have been possible without the support of my wife Anita. I would also like to thank Tom Riley, who edited this book. Tom was my former student at the New York School of the Bible and has now become my colleague. He is currently Dean and Instructor at the New York Institute for Biblical Studies in Staten Island.

I also want to thank my longtime and close friend, Van Misheff, who has edited and published my three former books, Even now, he has had a hand in the publication of this book. His encouragement and friendship has been indispensable.

However, I want to reserve the greatest gratitude for my Lord and Savior Jesus Christ who, through my many tears and struggles, has opened my eyes to the riches of His Word.

Table of Contents
Chapter Summaries

PART I ~
A RATIONALE FOR APOLOGETICS AND THIS DEFENSE OF THE BIBLE

Even if the postmodern age calls for new ways of doing apologetics, the biblical methods should not be abandoned. The authors of the Bible make references to reasons for faith far more than most would suspect.

Biblical faith does not require a leap into the darkness. Instead, it forbids such a leap in favor of faith based on evidence. However, Richard Dawkins insists that faith is mindless. Sadly, there are some Christians who erroneously defend such an evidence-less faith.

Both the negative and positive forms of apologetics are Scriptural.

PART II ~
WHY BELIEVE
The BIBLE IS GOD'S WORD

WHY BELIEVE
The BIBLE IS GOD'S WORD

WHY BELIEVE
THE BIBLE IS GOD'S WORD

In the Hebrew Scriptures, whenever we see a reference to the Crucifixion, we also find a cryptic indication that the Crucified will rise again. Could this be by chance? It would be like rolling the dice eight times in a row and coming up with snake eyes each time.

There is a wealth of evidence that our knowledge external to the Bible – scientific, historical, psychological – accords with the Bible. From where could the Bible have acquired such knowledge if it didn't come from God!

The Babylonian Talmud's compilation was completed around 550 AD. It is the definitive rabbinic commentary on the Hebrew Scriptures, and it includes many derogatory sayings against Jesus. However, it also acknowledges facts that support the Christian faith.

PART III ~
INTERNAL CONSISTENCY OF THE BIBLE

INTRODUCTION

HESITANT ABOUT PROOFS AND APOLOGETICS?

Many question the value of apologetics, the discipline that provides rational "reasons to believe" for the Christian faith, and ultimately, for the Bible upon which our faith rests. However, we are instructed to defend the faith (*Jude 3*) and also to provide the reasons why we believe:

- In your hearts honor Christ the Lord as holy, always being prepared to make a defense to anyone who asks you for a reason for the hope that is in you; yet do it with gentleness and respect. (*1 Peter 3:15*).

A friend of mine commented that he's seen many people come to faith without any evidences or rational grease to lubricate this transition. Although this may be true, many others require a mental shoehorn to ease them past the doubts and intellectual objections.

I am not trying to argue for a salvation-by-rationality. Instead, Salvation is clearly of the Lord (*2 Timothy 2:24-26*) and entirely His free gift to us (*Ephesians 2:8-9*). However, He has demonstrated that He's not at all averse to using argumentation (*Acts 17:2-4; 18:4*), wisdom (*2 Timothy 3:15*) and evidences (*John 10:37; 20:31; Acts 1:3; 2:22*) to accomplish His miraculous work of Salvation.

Many have testified that the absence of a rationale for the faith allowed them to stray away. In the *Search for the Truth* periodical, scientist and creationist Bruce Malone writes:

"Prior to graduation from college, I had not once been shown any of the scientific evidence for creation either in school or in church. Little wonder, that by the time I started my career [as a chemist], God had little relevance in my life. It wasn't as though I had any animosity toward God or religion. It simply held no relevance to the world around me. This should be no surprise when the subject never came up in school and everything seemed to be explained without reference to a Creator."

However, the rational underpinning of the faith is also of paramount importance to those of us who already believe. I myself have been blessed with weakness-of-faith. By nature, I am fretful and doubting. Whenever a doubt would enter into my anxious thoughts, I was never able to merely dismiss it. It was like an infection that had to be lanced and drained, or else it would spread. I couldn't make-believe that it wasn't there. It was just too painful. In this way, Christ coerced me to deal with these issues.

Although this process had been quite painful, I can now thank God for my weaknesses, because through them He created in me understanding, assurance and strength. He has comforted me with His knowledge and has privileged me with something very precious that I can pass on to others (*2 Corinthians 1:4*). Consequently, I now enjoy going to atheist meetings and blogging in hostile environs. These evangelistic opportunities give me far more pleasure than playing tennis.

Although making rational defenses of the Faith – "Apologetics" – might not be expressing the Faith itself, they serve as a protective shield for our spiritual life in the same way that the earth's atmosphere shields us from dangerous rays, while allowing the beneficial rays to enter our lives (*2 Corinthians 10:4-5*). To ignore this shield is to ignore the Bible, which gives us so many warnings against the power of bad teachings which corrupt faith and draw many away from Christ.

It was for this reason that Paul required that elders possess a mastery of Scripture so that they would be able to refute false teachings that were leading people away from Christ:

- For an overseer… must hold firm to the trustworthy word as taught, so that he may be able to give instruction in sound doctrine and also to rebuke those who contradict it. For there are many who are insubordinate, empty talkers and deceivers, especially those of the circumcision party. They must be silenced, since they are upsetting whole families... (*Titus 1:7-1*)

Paul also warned that false philosophies, when embraced, also possessed such power (*Colossians 2:8, 18-23*). Jesus wasn't a fear-monger, but He too warned His disciples against the corrosive doctrines of the religious leadership (*Matthew 7:15; Mark 8:15*).

When we ignore Apologetics, we ignore the welfare of the Church and the commands of Scripture to defend the Faith (*Jude 3*). Many had been devastated by reading the "*Da Vinci Code.*" The author, Dan Brown, suggested that the Bible was merely the product of political infighting, and that many other equally substantial candidates for canonical inclusion, (i.e. the Gnostic Gospels), all were written at least one hundred years after the crucifixion and had been arbitrarily rejected. Fortunately, a number of able apologists came forth with books and DVDs to address this potent threat.

Furthermore, Apologetics isn't simply defensive – taking captive the challenges that come to us from Science, Psychology, History, and Biblical Criticism – it is also offensive and elucidates faith-building and God-glorifying Biblical and even extra-Biblical material. For example, it illustrates how Christ has fulfilled prophecy. Jesus also prophesied to His struggling disciples about what would later occur so that "when it does happen, you will believe" (*John 14:28-29*). They needed corroborating evidences, and so do we! When we lack these evidences, we are easily muscled into silence by those who accuse: "What right do you Christians have to tell believers in other religions that you have the truth and they don't! That's just arrogance! How do you presume that your religious experiences are any more valid than theirs? They also have their revelations." If we can't argue that Christ is not only our life, but He's also the Truth – and there are many solid reasons to believe this – then their charge of "arrogance" remains.

Often I've heard people say—especially theistic evolutionists— that "The Bible isn't about proof but proclamation." Of course, it is about proclamation, but it's *also* about proof. *Psalm 19* declares that the creation points to its Creator:

- The heavens declare the glory of God, and the sky above proclaims his handiwork. Day to day pours out speech, and night to night reveals knowledge. There is no speech, nor are there words, whose voice is not heard. Their voice goes out through all the earth, and their words to the end of the world. (*Psalm 19:1-4*)

Scripture declares that God's creation speaks about Him. Therefore, when the skeptic demands that I show him proof of the Creation, I sometimes respond:

- We are surrounded by the proof. Wherever we look, we see evidence of our Creator. We see this evidence in life, DNA, and in every elegant, knowable, and immutable law of Science. We see Him in the sunrise, in the planets, and in the sunset. We see Him in life and even in our own conscience.

This evidence is so compelling that we are "without excuse" for not believing:

- For the wrath of God is revealed from heaven against all ungodliness and unrighteousness of men, who by their unrighteousness suppress the truth. For what can be known about God is plain to them, because God has shown it to them. For his invisible attributes, namely, his eternal power and divine nature, have been clearly perceived, ever since the creation of the world, in the things that have been made. So they are without excuse. (*Romans 1:18-20*)

Though I might be weak in faith and require more rational reassurances than most, we all are weak to some extent. Our faith is always under construction (*1 Peter 4:11*), and construction sites are not very pretty.

Sadly, I've heard many testimonies claiming that youth leaders were simply too ill-equipped to answer the youths' questions about the reasons for the faith. The youth have then concluded that there simply weren't any answers and left the Church.

Without the protective shield of evidences and proofs, we become highly vulnerable to the assaults of doubt. Jesus' crucifixion caused His disciples to doubt and flee. Yet, Jesus restored them through the compelling proofs of His resurrection (Acts 1:3). Conversely, a rejection of Apologetics becomes an invitation to hungry viruses to invade and to take us captive, instead of our fulfilling our mandate to take them captive:

- For the weapons of our warfare are not of the flesh but have divine power to destroy strongholds. We destroy arguments and every lofty opinion raised against the knowledge of God, and take every thought captive to obey Christ (*2 Corinthians 10:4-5*).

If we fail to take these thoughts captive, they will certainly take us captive. A little leaven (yeast) will leaven the entire loaf of bread (*Galatians 5:9*).

None of us are above doubting (*1 Corinthians10:13*). Jesus warned that the power of false teachings and signs can be so overwhelming that even His chosen ones could be deceived (*Matthew 24:11, 24*). Indeed, He will not allow this to happen. However, don't count on His protection if we reject one of His ordained means of defense.

Note: Most of Scripture references are from the English Standard Version (ESV) and New International Version (NIV) unless otherwise noted.

Chapter 1

APOLOGETICS IN A POSTMODERN AGE

While Theology tries to provide the Church with *what* we should believe, Apologetics attempts to come up with reasons for *why* we should believe. Admittedly, doing Apologetics in the postmodern West has not been very fruitful. There are probably many reasons for this. Perhaps the denial of spiritual truth leads the list. For many today, spirituality is simply a matter of what works or feels right for you. This has led many Christians to claim that the old methods no longer work and that we need new strategies including those that bypass rationality.

While there is nothing wrong with finding new methods, they must be supported Biblically. That being said, it may not be wise to discard the strategies that have been used in the past which relied on rational arguments. In fact, a rationalistic defense of the faith is part of the fabric of the entirety of Scripture.

Apologetics is not just a matter of a few isolated verses like *Jude 3, 1 Peter 3:15*, and *2 Corinthians 10:4-5*. All of Scripture rests squarely on a foundation of reasons for believing. For instance, Luke prefaces his Gospel with several of these reasons where he claims that he has thoroughly investigated what various eyewitnesses have reported and then has drawn up an orderly account:

- Therefore, since I myself have carefully investigated everything from the beginning, it seemed good also to me to write an orderly account for you, most excellent Theophilus, so that you may *know the certainty* of the things you have been taught. (*Luke 1:3-4*, emphasis added)

Luke was concerned about the evidential basis for the Faith, in the writing of his Gospel. He was clearly doing apologetics.

Likewise, the Apostle John, as an eyewitness to the earthly ministry of Jesus, assured the readers of his Gospel about his apologetic intent in a similar way:

- Jesus performed many other *signs* in the presence of his disciples, which are not recorded in this book. But *these are written that you may believe* that Jesus is the Messiah, the Son of God, and that by believing you may have life in his name. (*John 20:30-31*, emphasis added).

John's ultimate goal was for his readers to believe and to "have life in his name." However, the process wasn't magical. John understood that his readers needed food for their minds, reasons to support belief. Therefore, John provided evidence such as including his accounts of the miracles of Jesus. John, like Luke, used Apologetics to reach his audience.

Peter also insisted on the importance of evidence or reasons to believe. He wanted his readers to have a solid basis to believe certain truths and was not content to merely state these truths, as we see in his Epistle. Peter offered reasons for why the disciples should believe what he was saying:

- For we did not follow cleverly devised stories when we told you about the coming of our Lord Jesus Christ in power, but we were *eyewitnesses of his majesty*. He received honor and glory from God the Father when the voice came to him from the Majestic Glory, saying, "This is my Son, whom I love; with him I am well pleased." We ourselves *heard this voice* that came from heaven when we were with him on the sacred mountain. We also have the prophetic message as something completely reliable... (*2 Peter 1:16-19a*, emphasis added)

Peter cited the fact that they, the Apostles, were eyewitnesses to the things they were claiming. Yet, that wasn't all he did. He also cited the evidence of the "prophetic message"—Scripture. Thus we see, yet again, the way that Theology and Apologetics work together.

Finally, it is clear that none of the Apostles ever asked believers to take a blind leap of faith. As they understood it, faith had a powerful and necessary evidential basis.

Far from supposedly outgrowing our need for evidence, we still need the testimony of John and Luke and the other authors of Scripture to provide us with a rational basis for our faith. Therefore, while it might be important to explore new ways to reach our generation, we must not forget the old paths, which are potent sources of nourishment for God's people.

***

It has been argued that Apologetics alone cannot save anyone, which, of course, is true. If the Holy Spirit is not involved in the process, no amount of evidence can make a difference for the unbeliever. The renowned atheist and mathematician, Bertrand Russell, was once asked:

- Bertrand, what would you say to God if you encounter him after you die and he asks, "Bertrand, why didn't you believe?" Russell confidently responded, "There just wasn't enough evidence."

Here is the subtext of this reply:

- I am a rational person and rational people require evidence. The fault, therefore, wasn't with me but with You!

Richard Dawkins, perhaps the most famous atheist today, has taken it one step further BY claiming that *no evidence is possible to support belief in God!* In an interview hosted by Peter Boghossian, Dawkins was asked what it would take for him to believe in God. He dismissed the possibility that *any evidence was possible.* Even if Christ returned and he could see Him, Dawkins would have no way of knowing whether he was experiencing a hallucination or not.

However, if Dawkins were to use this logic consistently, he would also be depriving himself of any evidence for the existence of the universe. According to this line of thinking, the world as we know it might only be a dream. Why? Well, if Dawkins concludes that any appearance of God is an hallucination, why not also any appearance of the universe?

Nevertheless, Dawkins seems haunted by the idea that his dismissal of all possible evidence does not line up with the logic of Science. After all, if a theory can be proven false by evidence, it should also be amenable to evidential proof. Perhaps Dawkins is aware that he is playing fast and loose with the ways that the concepts of evidence and of science are generally understood.

In any event, Dawkins accurately reflects the state of mind of the unbeliever who is not being drawn by God. There is no amount of evidence that will change his or her mind. It is the heart of the unbeliever that must first be changed. Only then can the mind be truly responsive to the light of evidence.

Having said all that, it is important to understand that apologetics is, first of all, for us, His Church. We who believe need to be mentally assured of the truths of the Christian faith.

It is only with this assurance that the Lord has enabled me to stand and to confidently participate in many secular conversation groups.

Yet some Christians protest: "I don't need Apologetics. I just believe, and that is enough." Such a stance is inadequate as all believers need reasons for believing. For one thing, we are always changing as we are continually in the midst of a process whereby the Lord is refining and pruning our faith so that we can more ably serve Him.

- In this you rejoice, though now for a little while, if necessary, you have been grieved by various trials, so that the tested genuineness of your faith—more precious than gold that perishes though it is tested by fire—may be found to result in praise and glory and honor at the revelation of Jesus Christ. (*1 Peter 1:6-7*)

As our faith is "tested by fire", we will find that we need to dig deeper into the many reassurances that are available to us through the Word of God. Paul had warned us in Ephesians 6 that we *must* put on the entire Armor of God. This armor includes the sword of the Spirit, the Word of God. When we study the Word, we become more adept with the knowledge and the understanding of the reasons why we believe. Without this protection, there is a chink in our armor and we will fall.

- So, if you think you are standing firm, be careful that you don't fall! (*I Corinthians 10:12*)

John the Baptist was Israel's greatest prophet. He had heralded "the Lamb of God who takes away the sins of the world." He testified that he had seen the Holy Spirit descend upon Jesus at His baptism. Yet, when John was cast into prison, he too began to doubt whether Jesus was truly the Messiah:

- Now when John heard in prison about the deeds of the Christ, he sent word by his disciples and said to him, "Are you the one who is to come, or shall we look for another"? (*Matthew 11:2-3*)

How would Jesus answer these disciples of John? Would He say to them, "Just tell John to believe"? No! Instead, He told them to tell John about all the apologetic evidence for belief:

- And Jesus answered them, "Go and tell John what you hear and see: the blind receive their sight and the lame walk, lepers are cleansed and the deaf hear, and the dead are raised up, and the poor have good news preached to them." (*Matthew 11:4-5*).

If even John required evidential reassurances, then so do we! Later, Jesus indicated to the apostles that he was more than ready to provide the necessary reasons for them to believe. For example:

- "You heard me say to you, 'I am going away, and I will come to you.' If you loved me, you would have rejoiced, because I am going to the Father, for the Father is greater than I. And now I have *told you before it takes place*, so that when it does take place *you may believe*" (*John 14:28-29*, emphasis mine).

While some of us may require more evidence than others, we all require some measure of assurance. This chronic skeptic certainty did! However, searching for reassurance has produced in me a great confidence and, by His grace, boldness before a hostile world. It is this boldness that I hope to impart to my brethren.

Of course, as we have said before, apologetics *alone* cannot save. Furthermore, we need to remember as well that even the preaching of the Gospel of Christ cannot save. Salvation is not possible without the work of the Holy Spirit. Yet, we know and are convinced that the Spirit can use both preaching Christ and Apologetics to draw others to salvation.

Finally, it is hard to believe what is unbelievable. Secular authorities have done a good job in discrediting the Bible and, along with it, the Gospel message. Therefore, there is a great need to reclaim the trustworthiness and believability of this message and the Bible. That is what this book is about.

WORKS CITED:

Dawkins, Richard. "Richard Dawkins in Conversation with Peter Boghossian." 2013, www.youtube.com/watch?v=qNcC866sm7s.

Russell, Bertrand. "What to say when someone asks for proof of God's existence." *Christianity Today,* 22 January 2016, www.christiantoday.com/article/what.to.say.when.someone.asks.for.proof.of.gods.existence/77413.htm.

Chapter 2

OBJECTIONS TO APOLOGETICS

There shouldn't be any resistance to Apologetics – the reasons to believe that the Bible is God's Word. However, we often encounter this resistance. There are even some "Christians" who call themselves "Christian Agnostics." When asked why, they often respond that "No one can really know for certain. It's just a matter of blind faith."

Sadly, they don't seem to want to read the Bible for its evidences. However, it is obvious that many have come to know with certainty. If doubting Thomas had been told that there was no way for him to know of the resurrection for certain, he might have laughed and said, "I met the risen Savior." Even according to many skeptical historians, it is certain that the Apostles were convinced that they too had met the risen Jesus. This is also true for a great portion of the early Church who had witnessed Jesus and His miracles. (*1 Corinthians 15:5-8*)

We find the concern for an evidential basis for the faith woven into the fabric of Scripture. The *Book of Acts* is largely a book about the rationale for believing. Luke starts with an assertion that there are many "proofs" for the faith:

- He presented himself alive to them after his suffering by many proofs, appearing to them during forty days and speaking about the kingdom of God. (*Acts 1:3*)

Apollos was no exception. He too resorted to the proofs for the faith:

- When he [Apollos] arrived, he greatly helped those who through grace had believed, for he powerfully refuted the Jews in public, showing by the Scriptures that the

Christ [the Messiah] was Jesus. (*Acts 18:27-28*; Also Paul – *Acts 17:2-4; 18:4; 28:23-24*)

How had Apollos "greatly helped those who through grace had believed?" He "refuted the Jews in public, showing by the Scriptures that the Christ [the Messiah] was Jesus." He provided proof from the Hebrew Scriptures, demonstrating that Christians didn't have to close their minds to the facts in order to believe. Instead, Apollos showed that the evidence favored faith.

We too need to know why we believe, and not just what we should believe. Moses had this very concern when he was talking with God in the midst of the burning bush:

- Then Moses answered, "But behold, they will not believe me or listen to my voice, for they will say, 'The LORD did not appear to you.'" (*Exodus 4:1*)

Moses correctly understood that the Israelites would have to be convinced about the "why" question. They needed evidence, and God was prepared to provide that evidence:

- The LORD said to him, "What is that in your hand?" He said, "A staff." And he said, "Throw it on the ground." So he threw it on the ground, and it became a serpent, and Moses ran from it. But the LORD said to Moses, "Put out your hand and catch it by the tail"—so he put out his hand and caught it, and it became a staff in his hand— "that they may believe that the LORD, the God of their fathers, the God of Abraham, the God of Isaac, and the God of Jacob, has appeared to you." Again, the LORD said to him, "Put your hand inside your cloak." And he put his hand inside his cloak, and when he took it out, behold, his hand was leprous like snow. Then God said, "Put your hand back inside your cloak." So he put his hand back inside his cloak, and when he took it out, behold, it was restored like the rest of his flesh. "If they will not believe you," God said, "or listen to the first sign, they may believe the latter sign. If they will not believe even these two signs or listen to your voice, you shall take some water from the Nile and pour it on the dry ground, and the water that you shall take from the Nile will become blood on the dry ground" (*Exodus 4:2-9*).

God had provided Moses with a set of three miraculous proofs instead of ordering him to tell the Israelites, "Just believe." In fact, in the Bible blind belief is never commanded. Moses never told the Israelites, "Just believe." He didn't need to. Instead, he merely reminded them of God's miraculous workings on their behalf (*Deuteronomy 4:34-35*).

Biblical faith always rested upon reason and the evidences. In contrast, atheist and evolutionist Richard Dawkins disparages faith as the rejection of evidence and rationality:

- Faith is the great cop-out, the great excuse to evade the need to think and evaluate evidence. Faith is belief in spite of, even perhaps because of, the lack of evidence.

However, this isn't the Bible's idea of faith. Faith is not a blind leap into the abyss of mindlessness, but a willingness to step forth into the light of the evidence. This has been the consistent insistence of Scripture. When God asked Israel to love and obey Him, He never intended Israel to follow as a dumb beast. Instead, He asked them to recall the miracles that they had *all* witnessed:

Jesus directed His disciples to *not* believe without confirmatory evidence:

- If I am not doing the works of my Father, then do not believe me; but if I do them, even though you do not believe me, believe the works, that you may know and understand that the Father is in me and I am in the Father. (*John 10:37-38*)

According to Jesus, there were also other forms of confirmatory evidence:

- If I alone bear witness about myself, my testimony is not true. There is another who bears witness about me, and I know that the testimony that he bears about me is true. You sent to John, and he has borne witness to the truth. Not that the testimony that I receive is from man, but I say these things so that you may be saved. He was a burning and shining lamp, and you were willing to rejoice for a while in his light. But the testimony that I have is greater than that of John. For the works that the Father has given me to accomplish, the very works that I am doing, bear witness about me that the Father has sent me. And the Father who sent me has himself borne witness about me. (*John 5:31-37*)

Of course, Jesus' testimony is true, even without the evidences. However, His disciples were *not to regard it as true* without the supportive evidences. Jesus was merely harkening back to the Biblical principle that everything had to be established by at least two or three witnesses (*Deuteronomy 19:15*).

Jesus *never* asked His disciples to blindly believe but forbade it. The faith had to be based on the bedrock of fact. God had put into place rigorous requirements for anyone claiming to speak the words of God. They had to meet various demanding tests (*Deuteronomy 13:1-5; 18:20-22*).

Biblical faith was always meant to be a rational faith. Therefore, loving God wasn't just a matter of serving Him with our hearts but also with our "minds":

- Teacher, which is the great commandment in the Law?" And he said to him, "You shall love the Lord your God with all your heart and with all your soul and with all your mind. This is the great and first commandment. (*Matthew 22:36-38*)

Consequently, faith was never a matter of turning off our mind but of turning it on in service to our Lord. Faith doesn't require a mental lobotomy. In fact, this is *forbidden*. Instead, Jesus nurtured the faith of His disciples with proofs like prophetic fulfillments:

- I am telling you now before it happens, so that when it does happen you will believe that I am He. (*John 13:19; 14:28-29*)

Apostolic preaching was not of matter of "just believe." Instead, there was a consistent appeal to consider the evidences, as Peter had preached:

- Men of Israel, hear these words: Jesus of Nazareth, a man attested to you by God with mighty works and wonders and signs that God did through him in your midst, as you yourselves know. (*Acts 2:22*)

In light of the wealth of Biblical evidence that God gladly provides proof, how can these Christians deny the Bible's proof claims? Well, they can't, but they erroneously cite two verses to support their denial. After Jesus appeared to doubting Thomas, he believed and worshipped Jesus. However, He rebuked Thomas:

- Then Jesus told him, "Because you have seen me, you have believed; blessed are those who have not seen and yet have believed." (*John 20:29*)

Some Christians wrongly understand "blessed are those who have not seen and yet have believed," to mean "blessed are those who believe *without any evidence* for their belief." Such a misunderstanding represents a failure to appreciate the context:

1. Everyone was aware of Jesus' miracles, even His detractors. In many passages, the Jewish Talmud acknowledges that Jesus was a miracle worker, although they ascribe His miracles to Satan.

2. Thomas lived with Jesus two or three years and had seen many of His miracles – perhaps hundreds. He also had the testimonial evidence of his fellow disciples who had claimed that they had seen Jesus after His resurrection. Therefore, Thomas *already* had abundant evidence. Therefore, a lack of evidence wasn't his problem.

3. Thomas wasn't simply seeking evidence of the resurrection. He was *demanding* it, or else:

   - So the other disciples told him, "We have <u>seen</u> the Lord!" But he said to them, "Unless I <u>see</u> the nail marks in his hands and put my finger where the nails were, and put my hand into his side, I will not believe it." (*John 20:25*)

The disciples had claimed that they had "seen" Jesus. However, Thomas *refused* to accept their testimonies! Instead, he obstinately demanded to also "*see*," despite the fact that he already had adequate evidences.

In view of this, when Jesus affirmed the blessedness of "those who have not seen and yet have believed," He was affirming their willingness to believe without making *demands* of seeing for themselves. Jesus was also chastening Thomas' *demand* to *see* the resurrected Jesus and his *refusal* to believe without seeing.

The notion that Jesus would praise those who had faith *without* any solid reasons for faith contradicts all of Scripture, even His own say-so! It even contradicts the next verse:

- Jesus did many other miraculous signs in the presence of his disciples, which are not recorded in this book. But these are *written that you may believe* that Jesus is the Christ, the Son of God, and that by believing you may have life in his name. (*John 20:30-31*; emphasis added)

John acknowledged that belief must be accompanied by reasons to believe. Although the great majority of John's readers had not seen the Resurrection, this shouldn't prevent faith. According to John, there were other evidences for faith— namely the testimonial evidences that John and other eyewitnesses had provided. It would seem highly unlikely that John would have written against an evidence-based faith and then offer evidences so "that [they] may believe."

Some Christians cite a second verse in an attempt to prove that faith was intended as a mindless, evidence-less plunge into the darkness:

- Now faith is being sure of what we hope for and certain of what we do not see. (*Hebrews 11:1*)

However, this verse says nothing against an evidence-based faith. Even if faith is our *only* assurance—and it's not—faith is *not devoid* of the evidential foundations for belief, whether very personal or objective. For example, many of the following

29

examples of faith in *Hebrews 11* clearly depended upon prior evidences:

- By faith the people passed through the Red Sea as on dry land; but when the Egyptians tried to do so, they were drowned. (*Hebrews 11:29*)

Although the Israelites couldn't be certain that the piled-up waters of the Red Sea wouldn't engulf them as they passed through, they were convinced that God had miraculously led them out of Egypt and split the sea. They had seen the ten plagues that had devastated Egypt. Therefore, theirs wasn't an evidence-less, blind faith. Instead, it rested on an evidential foundation. God had already proved Himself to them. Nevertheless, they still had to pass through the sea by faith.

While it is true that the Bible commands us to have faith, *never* once does it command us to have faith in the absence of evidence. Although we are taught to walk by faith and not by sight (*2 Corinthians 5:7*), this walk presupposes the fact that we have *already* learned to "walk" based upon the work—the evidence—of the Spirit "as a guarantee" (*2 Corinthians 5:5-6*).

However, I must admit that *certain aspects* of the Christian life cannot rely directly on our knowledge and understanding. For example, I do not have any direct perceptions or evidences of heaven. However, I do believe in heaven because I believe in the Scriptures. But this belief in the Scriptures is not a blind belief or faith. It is a faith based upon the many evidences that the Bible is truly the Word of God. This is my very purpose for writing this book.

Faith is only irrational to those who are looking in from the outside, like Martians observing humans swaying and clapping to music. They may hear the musical notes, but, to Martian ears, they fail to come together in any meaningful way. In fact, the Martians might even seek to disparage the swaying and clapping as "mindless" and animalistic and use it as proof that humans are an inferior race, fit only for food consumption.

However, if the Martians were willing to examine us further they might better appreciate us. I think that the same thing pertains to those who are willing to examine the foundations of Biblical faith. Even more so, it also pertains to all of us of "little faith."

Chapter 3

APOLOGETICS CAN TAKE DIFFERENT FORMS

Apologetics is as big as the entire world of ideas. This is because challenges to the faith come from every direction and discipline. For example, out of the halls of science has come the Theory of Evolution. Out of biblical criticism has come various theories that claim that the Bible is just the product of human beings trying to make sense of their lives. As believers, if we fail to take these ideas captive, they will take us captive along with our faith.

One such theory, the Documentary Hypothesis put forth by Julius Wellhausen, had taken me captive before I had entered seminary. This theory has no room for God. Instead, it claimed that the Hebrew Scriptures, the Pentateuch in particular, were merely the result of editors cutting-and-pasting from various manuscripts over a period of hundreds of years.

However, I decided that I wouldn't allow such skepticism to tamper with my faith. Instead, I would tuck it away into the recesses of my mind until I'd have the resources to confront it. However, our minds don't work that way. Instead, whenever I would read the Bible, the arrows of this theory would secretly puncture my confidence, sowing doubts and discomforts. Consequently, I began to read the Bible less and less.

Fortunately, I was given a copy of *Survey of Old Testament Introductions* by Gleason Archer, which conclusively exposed the fallacies of Wellhausen. Consequently, I cried my way through this ordinarily dry book. Archer had restored my Bible back to me.

***

Apologetics can take many different forms. For the sake of simplicity, I will divide them into two forms – negative and positive.

The positive approach offers evidences; the negative answers the challenges with logic and reason. The negative is the more offensive and direct of the two. Jesus Himself used both. When the religious leadership accused Him of casting out demons by the hand of Satan, He retorted with an example of negative apologetics:

- Knowing their thoughts, he said to them, "Every kingdom divided against itself is laid waste, and no city or house divided against itself will stand. And if Satan casts out Satan, he is divided against himself. How then will his kingdom stand? (*Matthew 12:25-26*)

If Satan is at war against himself and his minions, his kingdom would self-destruct. Therefore, the allegation of the Pharisees was not reasonable (logical). Adding to their logical problems, the very next verse suggests that they too had been encouraging the deliverance ministry among their own without a concern that they might also be tapping into the power of Satan. It seems like their charging Jesus with a satanic partnership, without likewise examining their own people, smacked of hypocrisy.

On numerous occasions, Jesus pointed out their hypocrisy through a logical critique (negative apologetics). The Pharisees often charged Jesus with violating the Sabbath by healing during it. For instance, after a healing at a synagogue, the leadership criticized Him of violating the Sabbath. To this, Jesus responded:

- You hypocrites! Does not each of you on the Sabbath untie his ox or his donkey from the manger and lead it away to water it? And ought not this woman, a daughter of Abraham whom Satan bound for eighteen years, be loosed from this bond on the Sabbath day? (*Luke 13:15-16*)

Were they truly hypocrites? Yes! Jesus logically demonstrated that they were using a double standard – one standard against Him and another to allow them to take care of their animals on the Sabbath. Besides, healing the woman was of far greater importance than watering the animals.

This type of logical critique is so powerful that it allows no come-back. Instead, the leadership was ashamed of themselves. (Sometimes love requires shaming!)

Elsewhere, Jesus again pointed out their hypocrisy in their use of two different standards. They accused Jesus of healing on the Sabbath, while they gladly circumcised on the Sabbath:

- If on the Sabbath a man receives circumcision, so that the Law of Moses may not be broken, are you angry with me because on the Sabbath I made a man's whole body well? Do not judge by appearances, but judge with right judgment. (*John 7:23-24*)

By regarding only one verse out of the many on the subject, they were not rendering a superficially correct but prejudicial judgment. Often, Jesus accused them of either misusing or not even knowing Scripture:

- But Jesus answered them, "You are wrong, because you know neither the Scriptures nor the power of God. For in the resurrection they neither marry nor are given in marriage, but are like angels in heaven. And as for the resurrection of the dead, have you not read what was said to you by God: 'I am the God of Abraham, and the God of Isaac, and the God of Jacob'? He is not God of the dead, but of the living." (*Matthew 22:29-32*)

34

In contrast, the "positive approach", offers evidences and proofs but does not immediately silence the opposition. For example, take your own testimony. While some will find it impressive and even inspiring, others will dismiss it, saying:

- Why should I believe you, or
- Buddhists' claim that meditation has changed their lives, or
- Muslims claim that Allah has given them meaning and purpose.

Whatever you say, they can always offer counter "evidence." If you say that Jesus changes lives, they can retort, "Jesus also ruins lives." If you say that Christianity served as the impetus for the resurgence of Science, they will say that, "Christianity has been the source of ignorance and repression," and might cite how Christians have impeded fetal tissue research.

In short, when you are confronted by a hostile militant and decide that it is better to hold your ground than to wipe the dust off of your feet, it is generally more profitable to use negative apologetics. This is what I often use to address the militants.

"Negative apologetics" come in many forms. After I had posted a brief essay on Facebook, an atheist reiterated the same tiring challenge: "Well, you first have to prove your god exists!"

If you have tried to present proofs to militant atheists, you know how futile this can be. No matter how weighty your proof, the atheist can still quibble with it. This might not reflect a problem with your proof, but their unmovable commitment to their own faith. It also might reflect a problem with all proofs in general. However strong they might be, they are never airtight or unassailable.

Rather than engaging in this frustrating process, in many cases I've opted to place the burden of proof on the atheist: "First prove that you exist! This will prove to me that it is even worthwhile for me to even attempt to prove that God exists." Of course, they never can prove this to my satisfaction. The following dialogue illustrates this fact:

ATHEIST: You still have not shown me any evidence that god exists.

ME: Well, if you prove you exist, I'll prove God exists.

ATHEIST: I asked you first!

ME: That's true, but if you are just a computer spewing out messages, I don't have any obligation to you.

ATHEIST: Daniel, do you honestly think that there is a direct comparison between whether I exist, and whether god or Jesus exists? Clearly you have more evidence for me existing than for God or Jesus.

ME: Then prove you exist! Prove that you are not simply a bio-chemical robot or that you are not just an illusion as a monistic Buddhist would claim. Consistent with this, please define your use of the word "I." What is this thing you call "I"?

ATHEIST: You are just unable to prove that God exists.

ME: No! I am just presenting you with an object lesson. If you are unable to prove that you exist, you are in no position to demand that I prove that God exists. Besides, if I can successfully quibble about your existence, I trust that you will also be able to quibble with any solid evidence I offer in favor of God's existence.

You might ask, "Why even engage in such an argument?" Perhaps this argument will fail to show him the hypocrisy of his demand for more proof of God's existence than even for his own. However, there are others reading these exchanges on Facebook. It is my prayer that it might sow valuable seeds in the thinking of others.

However, negative apologetics can be used more effectively. When I have done open-air evangelism, scoffers will assault me with a series of charges. One scoffer yelled, "This is no way to be absolutely sure of any of this stuff."

While it might be tempting to offer evidences against this challenge, a question is often the best way to answer to a militant opponent. I therefore responded, "Are you absolutely sure?" If he says he is, I respond:

- How is it that you can be absolutely sure while you absolutely deny that I can be absolutely sure? Sounds like a double-standard to me.

Nine times out of ten, this will silence the scoffer. However, if he answers, "No, I am not sure," I will simply respond, "Why then are you making such a claim if you are not sure!"

Many others insist, "There is no such thing as absolute truth." I simply ask:

- Is your statement absolutely true?

Once again, if he answers, "Yes," I point out that he just contradicted himself, because if there is no absolute truth, then his own statement cannot be absolutely true.

There are many variations of these illogical challenges. For instance, some say, "The only truth is change itself." Therefore, I ask, "Then doesn't that mean that the 'truth' of your statement is changing?" If he admits to this, then I merely respond that his statement is therefore meaningless, since it too will change in the next day.

Sometimes our negative apologetic might require a bit more information to expose the contradiction. Often, skeptics will make moral charges against our faith and God. For example, in a *Time Magazine* debate, atheist and evolutionist, Richard Dawkins, was asked (Dawkins, 55):

- "Do humans have a different moral significance than do cows?"

To this, Dawkins responded, "Humans have more moral responsibility, perhaps because they are capable of reasoning."

However, if our moral responsibility depends on being "capable of reasoning," then some humans are more morally culpable than others. Why? Because some are able to reason better than others! Therefore, before the court can pass judgment on the guilty party, they should administer an IQ test to determine the extent of the punishment. Absurd, right?

However, Dawkins has a greater problem. Prior to this, Dawkins admitted, "I don't believe that there is hanging out there, anywhere, something called good and something called evil."

This makes Dawkins a moral relativist. He doesn't believe that morality has any existence outside of our thinking. Therefore, morality is just something that *we* create. This makes morality relative to the individual and society. Consequently, without a higher, unchanging, and objective basis, morality is subjective. It's just what we feel or decide it to be. This means that Dawkins cannot say that his morality is more valid than Hitler's morality. However, in *The God Delusion*, Dawkins famously claimed (Dawkins, page 51):

- The God of the Old Testament is arguably the most unpleasant character in all fiction: jealous and proud of it; a petty, unjust, unforgiving control-freak; a vindictive, bloodthirsty ethnic cleanser; a misogynistic, homophobic, racist, infanticidal, genocidal, filicidal, pestilential, megalomaniacal, sadomasochistic, capriciously malevolent bully.

Had Dawkins merely stated, "This is just the way I feel about God," there would be no logical problem. However, coming from a position of moral relativism or subjectivism, he cannot coherently pronounce an objective indictment that something is absolutely wrong.

In order to claim that Hitler or God was wrong, we would need to base our indictment upon an objective standard. When, as Probation Officer, I wrote up charges against a probationer, I had to use objective language coming directly from the State Penal Law book. I could not charge a probationer with something that I merely felt was a crime. Instead, it had to be written in the Probation Code Book.

However, Dawkins admits there is no code book, no objective or absolute moral laws that can be broken. In fact, whenever a moral relativist - and all atheists are essentially moral relativists - brings a moral indictment against Christianity, I remind them that they cannot bring an objective charge without an objective standard. With their subjective self-based morality they cannot logically bring a moral charge against anybody.

Therefore, when the atheist charges, "Your God is a genocidal maniac!, I simply respond, "What's wrong with that?" As a moral relativist, there can be nothing *objectively* wrong with genocide!

However, for us, this doesn't end the question. We want to be able to *know* and to *explain* why our God is not "petty, unjust, unforgiving control-freak; a vindictive, bloodthirsty ethnic cleanser; a misogynistic, homophobic…" as Dawkins has claimed.

Why? Because confidence in our faith and our walk depends upon successfully grappling with these issues! This requires us to meditate on the Word both day and night (*Joshua 1:8*; *Psalm 1*), so that we can offer (to ourselves, first of all) positive evidences against the doubts and challenges to our faith.

This brings us to the following chapters of this book, were we deal with positive Apologetics, the evidences that the Bible is the Word of God.

I hope, at this point, that you are still following me through this prolonged introduction to the world of Apologetics. We will now change gears and look exclusively at the evidences of the Bible.

I am convinced that this question of the origin of the Bible, whether of God or of man, is the most important question that confronts apologetics. If the Bible is fully God-breathed (*2 Timothy 3:16-17*), then it can become the foundation of our entire lives. If, instead, it is the word of man, then why bother with it!

You might protest that, "The Bible must be the word of man, since, in so many ways (vocabulary, writing style, the personal experiences of the authors), it contains the fingerprints of its authors." In fact, if this is your protest, you are in good company. In a debate with Jordan Peterson, Sam Harris was adamant that the Bible is just a human creation. (Jordan Peterson/Sam Harris Debate) (www.youtube.com)

Harris takes his analysis one step forward. He argues that those who live by the Bible are closed minded, dangerous, and resistant to reasoning and to any new data. Actually, if Harris is correct about the Bible as a collection of strictly human documents, then he has a good point. This is why we have to be convinced that God is able to sovereignly work through human freewill choices to accomplish His purposes.

"Rubbish?" The Bible is littered with examples of how God led individuals, kings, and even nations to do His bidding as they lived their lives and made their freewill and culpable choices. How? That answer resides with our Lord and His glory. But rest assured that nothing is too hard for the Creator and Sustainer of this universe!

The rest of this book is an attempt to answer, with positive evidences, Harris and the many other voices that dismiss the Bible as the Word of God. These evidences might not be able to change Harris' mind, but I'm hoping that they will be able to fortify the Church against the increasing attacks.

WORKS CITED

Archer, Gleason, *Survey of Old Testament Introductions,* (Chicago: Moody Press, 1964)

Dawkins, Richard, *Times Magazine* debate (11/13/06, p. 55.)

Dawkins, Richard, *The God Delusion*, (NYC: Bantam Books, 2006)

Jordan Peterson/Sam Harris Debate,
www.youtube.com/watch?time_continue=5995&v=jey_CzIOfYE

Chapter 4

PERSONAL EVIDENCE: WHY THE BIBLE IS SO PRECIOUS TO ME

There are those who say that Christ doesn't make a difference. They claim that Christians act the same way as others and that Christ doesn't change lives. However, I **know** otherwise!

I have found that the Bible contains transforming and empowering wisdom, a wisdom that has brought me all sorts of blessings. For example, anger and hatred are tyrants that override reason and even self-interest. Yet, I knew that hatred is wrong. I even knew that it torments its prey. Nevertheless, it consumed me, as I watched powerlessly against it. Even its "arguments" were persuasive. They felt so right. Hatred placed its own lens over my eyes, and I saw only red.

However, I remembered the Word of God:

- Let love be genuine. Abhor what is evil; hold fast to what is good... Bless those who persecute you; bless and do not curse them... Live in harmony with one another. Do not be haughty, but associate with the lowly. Never be wise in your own sight. Repay no one evil for evil, but give thought to do what is honorable in the sight of all. If possible, so far as it depends on you, live peaceably with all. Beloved, never avenge yourselves, but leave it to the wrath of God, for it is written, "Vengeance is mine, I will repay, says the Lord." To the contrary, "if your enemy is hungry, feed him; if he is thirsty, give him something to drink; for by so doing you will heap burning coals on his head." Do not be overcome by evil, but overcome evil with good. (*Romans 12:9, 14, 16-21*)

His Word came upon me with such force and conviction that it drove the hatred away. The bully yelped helplessly as it fled. Instead, I was left rejoicing at the great privilege to love others and to "overcome evil with good."

It is no wonder Scripture informs us that loving God is about embracing and obeying His teachings:

- If you keep my commandments, you will abide in my love, just as I have kept my Father's commandments and abide in his love. These things I have spoken to you, that my joy may be in you, and that your joy may be full. This is my commandment, that you love one another as I have loved you. Greater love has no one than this, that someone lay down his life for his friends. You are my friends if you do what I command you. (*John 15:10-14*)

Keeping His teachings is our cure, our protective shield and the source of blessings. It even rescues us from destruction:

- Only be strong and very courageous [Joshua], being careful to do according to all the law that Moses my servant commanded you. Do not turn from it to the right hand or to the left, that you may have good success wherever you go. This Book of the Law shall not depart from your mouth, but you shall meditate on it day and night, so that you may be careful to do according to all that is written in it. For then you will make your way prosperous, and then you will have good success. (*Joshua 1:7-8*)

Consequently, we are instructed to "meditate on it day and night."

I am a man of many flaws, and they can be deeply troubling. However, I have learned something of even greater significance – that our Lord brings strength out of our ongoing weaknesses, as Paul had learned:

- Three times I pleaded with the Lord about this [affliction] that it should leave me. But he said to me, "My grace is sufficient for you, for my power is made perfect in weakness." Therefore I will boast all the more gladly of my weaknesses, so that the power of Christ may rest upon me. For the sake of Christ, then, I am content with weaknesses, insults, hardships, persecutions, and calamities. For when I am weak, then I am strong. (*2 Corinthians 12:8-10*)

I too have learned to boast in my weaknesses. They continue to humble me, trampling down my pride. These weaknesses also draw me closer to my Savior through His Word, which ministers so powerfully to me, through His blessed Spirit.

All of this has been made possible by the wisdom of the Living Word of God. Its wisdom has provided me with exactly what I had needed. Here are just a few more examples:

I am always second-guessing myself, wondering, "Did I say the right thing? ...Did I say it with the wrong motives? … Could I have said it more effectively?" Although this perfectionistic preoccupation can promote self-improvement, it can also drive me crazy. I needed to lay it aside before it laid me out, and the Holy Spirit did this for me through applying Scripture to my life:

- I have been crucified with Christ and I no longer live, but Christ lives in me. The life I live in the body, I live by faith in the Son of God, who loved me and gave himself for me. (*Galatians 2:20*)

What a relief! My failures were no longer my own. They belonged to my Savior who promised that He would work all things for my good (*Romans 8:28*), even my worst failures, nightmares, and my worst humiliations! I was now free to fail. Not that failures no longer hurt, but I now know who will lift me out of my discouragement (*1 Corinthians 10:12-13*), and He has proved this to me repeatedly. Consequently, Biblical truth allows me to constructively face my challenges without being overwhelmed by them.

We are also self-obsessed with questions of our goodness and worthiness. One of the greatest threats to our psychological well-being is the dread of not being worthy. This might take the form of a deep and abiding sense of shame, insecurity, or inadequacy. We might worry that we are not even worthy of *God*. Therefore, it is such a relief to realize that *none* of us are worthy. We are all sinners who need the Savior:

- There is no one righteous, not even one; there is no one who understands, no one who seeks God. All have turned away, they have together become worthless; there is no one who does good, not even one. (*Romans 3:10-12*)

This had certainly been true of me. Even though I attempted to suppress this truth of my moral inadequacy before God, it would continue to resurface to my great shame. I tried to beat back the ugly truth with self-assertions that I was really a good and loving person. I was engaged in a costly war with myself, and the result was desperation and depression.

Instead of deriving my sense of worthiness or adequacy from myself, I needed to find it from another source, and Scripture informed me that Jesus is that source:

- God made him who had no sin to be sin for us, so that in him we might become the righteousness of God. (*2 Corinthians 5:21*)

46

I could begin to accept the fact that I am entirely unworthy, because, in the eyes of my Savior, I am now entirely righteous. I could now face the once-shaming truths about myself and take responsibility for my behavior, because I have been assured of my ultimate worth before Him!

My wife can now charge me with being insensitive, and I can readily apologize. We're restored! Others can regard me negatively, but that's okay because I am now defined, not by what others might think, but by what my Savior thinks. Yes, it still hurts, but it no longer devastates me.

For the longest time, I had been feeling condemned. Even after Christ came into my life, I still had that sense. My feelings were so forceful that everything else – even Scripture – appeared as merely hollow words in comparison. I felt that even God condemned me! Finally, Scripture broke through, took hold of my self-contempt, and tore it apart, like a lion tearing apart red meat. What a consolation it has been to learn that:

- Therefore, there is now no condemnation for those who are in Christ Jesus. (*Romans 8:1*)

This taught me conclusively that my feelings of condemnation and rejection had nothing to do with God rejecting me, but just my own aberrant reactions! I could now laugh at these once terrifying feelings, knowing that they have nothing to do with my ultimate status! It's like receiving a letter saying that there has been a warrant issued for your arrest. However, upon reading it more closely, you find that the letter is actually addressed to someone else.

Many say, *"Well, I'm glad Christ worked for you, but many find consolation through psychotherapy."* It didn't work for me. I had seen five highly recommended psychologists, and each left me worse off than I was before.

Yes, they all affirmed that I was "okay," even superior, but I could never believe them, at least, not at the core of my being. I knew what my feelings were telling me, and they talked with a greater authority than the psychologists. I just *knew* I wasn't "okay."

Their affirmations rolled off my back as if it was made of Teflon. Perhaps this was because I had been giving myself false affirmations all my life. I told myself I was the greatest but actually felt that I was the least. After a while, these affirmations became no more than an addiction. I needed them but got little out of them. However, having believed them (and this distorted my thinking and perceptions), they alienated me from reality, wisdom, and honest relationship. Because I perceived the world through my distorted self-affirmations, I also regarded others through this grid. They were either superior or inferior to me. If they were seen as "superior," I resented them. If "inferior," I disdained them.

However, these affirmations bore little resemblance to reality, while I subsequently found that the Biblical affirmations brought me in touch with a deeper reality. Now, perceiving myself as an object of God's mercy, I began to regard others with mercy.

Besides, our sense of okay-ness requires *more* than the affirmation of other people. They all say different things, and every experience (every success and every failure) sings a different song. Which was I to believe? Therefore, to base my worth on either the opinions of others or on my socially approved accomplishments meant that my worth was like the stock market – booming, crashing, and the cause of constant instability and insecurity.

Besides, if my well-being depended on the opinions of others, I would resent them when they failed to project the "right" opinions of me. This would also place enormous pressure on them.

Not only does Scripture tell us what to believe, it tells us what to avoid. It is not simply that certain acts are regarded as "sin." These same acts also destroy. Sin is worse than eating junk food. The latter just destroys the body. Sin destroys everything about us. It contaminates our thinking and passions (*Romans 1:21-32*). For one thing, as a result of sin, we carry around unresolved guilt and shame. We even project our shame and self-contempt on others, convinced that others regard us in the same way we feel about ourselves. However, Scripture relieves us of these blinding burdens:

- If we confess our sins, he is faithful and just and will forgive us our sins and purify us from all unrighteousness. If we claim we have not sinned, we make him out to be a liar and his word has no place in our lives. (*1 John 1:9-10*)

Instead, we often try to cover over this problem with a variety of palliatives – successes, sex, drugs, popularity. However, there is nothing that gives the relief and cleansing the way that confession does.

What makes the affirmations of Scripture so powerful *and* so life transforming? For one thing, they illuminate what had been shadowy and confusing. In the hand of the Holy Spirit, Scripture tore me down so it could build me up on a solid foundation. It penetrated the blind spots created by my defensive mechanisms.

Once I began to understand myself in the light of Scripture, I found that I began to understand others. With the assurance of God's love and forgiveness, I could begin to face myself. As I saw my needs and insecurities (I had previously run from these and denied them), I could also see those of other people. As I began to face my denials and rationalizations, I began to understand the same defensive maneuverings I saw in others. As I received God's compassion for me, I could more readily extend it to others.

While Scripture is foolishness and contemptible to the one whose eyes haven't been opened (*1 Corinthians 2:14*), it is the scalpel in the hand of the Holy Spirit. It cuts deeply to remove malignant tumors (*Hebrews 4:12*) – attitudes and ideas that fail to accord with holiness. Such cuts are always painful (*Hebrews 12:5-11*), but they identify and remove cancers that threaten our well-being. They expose jealousy and provide the perfect antidote – the promise of His rest:

- All things are yours, whether Paul or Apollos or Cephas or the world or life or death or the present or the future-- all are yours. (*1 Corinthians 3:21-22*)

In light of God's assurances that He wants to eternally give us the world, jealousy had to take a back seat. I myself had been jealous, even of the spiritual successes of others, convinced that they would receive heavenly reward and recognition, and I wouldn't. However, Scripture assures us that all of God's people are one, and "all things" would be ours. We have become joint heirs with our Savior (*Romans 8:17*).

This is just what I needed to know. This truth stomped all the vitality out of my jealousy. I now rejoice as others rejoice!

Through the Scriptures, I have even come to know my Savior in a more personal way. On top of my decades of serious depression, I began to experience panic attacks. These left me utterly devastated. I was so tormented that I could barely carry on a conversation or even read the Bible. I could hardly make it through the day, and to believe that God loved me was beyond my grasp.

However, despite my profound doubts, I had no other place to turn. So I would continue to make feeble attempts at prayer and Bible reading. But even when I succeeded at reading the Bible, I could only understand the simplest statements.

Nevertheless, on numerous occasions, God spoke to me. For example, on one occasion, while reading the phrase, "And God heard him," a light exploded upon my tormented mind. The depression and panic were instantly driven away. I looked for them, but they were nowhere to be found.

Yet, they returned on the following day, but something had changed. I knew that God had *also* heard me and that He would keep on hearing me! I therefore knew that I was in His hands, despite my pathetic situation.

The Lord continued to reveal Himself to me in this manner over the next year, but these transformative experiences ceased entirely 35 years ago. I wish I could say that I had mastered the technique to bring on these electrifying encounters, but there is no technique for them, just the sovereign all-knowing workings of my Savior.

Indeed, the Lord continues to speak to me through His Word, but not in such a dramatic way. Why not? Because He prefers us to walk by faith and not by sight or by miraculous visitations (*2 Corinthians 5:7*). I now trust that He knows what is best for us.

Westerners have invented a new god, a god who is non-judgmental and non-punitive. Momentarily, this god might feel comfortable. However, once we have suffered victimization, our thoughts turn to justice, even revenge. Therefore, it is so liberating to know that we have a God who cares deeply about justice:

- If it is possible, as far as it depends on you, live at peace with everyone. Do not take revenge, my friends, but leave room for God's wrath, for it is written: "It is mine to avenge; I will repay," says the Lord. On the contrary: "If your enemy is hungry, feed him; if he is thirsty, give him something to drink" [Proverbs 25]…Do not be overcome by evil, but overcome evil with good. (*Romans 12:18-21*)

It is only because we have the assurance that God will bring justice (also through the legal systems He has ordained – (*Romans 13:1-4*) and know the undeserved love of god for us that we can devote ourselves to love. Without knowing these things, revenge would become a way of life.

When I read about the estimated 170,000 Christians being murdered yearly simply because they are Christians, I want to grab a machine gun or suicide belt and right the wrongs. But my Lord informs me that He has a better way. He'll deal with it! Instead, I should pray, love my enemies, and address the wrongs with righteous means. How liberating and personally enhancing!

This represents just a *small* sampling of the ways that God and His truth have infiltrated His people to bring us new life. Volumes can be written on this subject. Jesus had taught:

- "If you hold to my teaching, you are really my disciples. Then you will know the truth, and the truth will set you free." (*John 8:31-32*)

Not only has He set us free from sin and its various penalties, He has also set us free from so many things that have kept us in prison – fears, lusts, rationalizations, denials, addiction to self-affirmations, and many forms of self-deceptions.

From where does such wisdom come? I have become convinced that it must come from God through His Word.

Chapter 5

THE IMPACT OF THE BIBLE

In the last chapter, I presented my testimonies regarding the transforming power of God's Word by the Spirit. These testimonies serve as poignant reminders of our Lord and how He has impacted our lives through the Word. They are also useful evangelistic tools. However, far more is needed, as I hope these questions will show us:

- Perhaps the change I had experienced had little to do with the truth of the Bible?
- Perhaps it was just a product of my growing confidence with a sprinkle of wisdom, which is also available through other traditions?
- Perhaps my miraculous experiences in the Word were the results of my psychological needs?

Besides, these questions were compounded by the fact that others would automatically dismiss my testimonies saying, "Why should I value what you claim. I've also talked to Jews and Buddhists who also claim that they have been changed. Why should I regard your claim and dismiss theirs?"

All of these painful questions coerced me to dig deeper (*1 Corinthians14:20*). I already understood that a robust Christian life required more than just experiences but also a direct encounter with Scripture. The Psalms encourage us:

- Oh, taste and see that the LORD is good! Blessed is the man who takes refuge in him! Oh, fear the LORD, you his saints, for those who fear him have no lack! (*Psalm 34:8-9*)

To take refuge in the Lord is to trust in Him through obedience to His Word. Psalm 1 reveals the fate of the man who meditates on the Word day and night:

- He is like a tree planted by streams of water that yields its fruit in its season, and its leaf does not wither. In all that he does, he prospers. (*Psalm 1:3*)

Paul also promised that when we immerse ourselves in the Scriptures, people will observe positive changes:

- Until I come, devote yourself to the public reading of Scripture, to exhortation, to teaching…Practice these things, immerse yourself in them, so that all may see your progress. Keep a close watch on yourself and on the teaching. Persist in this, for by so doing you will save both yourself and your hearers. (*1 Timothy 4:13-16*)

Meanwhile, Jesus taught that to follow the word of the spiritually blind, is to suffer loss:

- Can a blind man lead a blind man? Will they not both fall into a pit? A disciple is not above his teacher, but everyone when he is fully trained will be like his teacher. (*Luke 6:39-40*)

To be "fully trained" in the Word is to bear the Spirit's fruit of obedience. It is encouraging to see how fidelity to this ancient book has borne positive results even in the modern world of today.

However, can we see this dynamic play itself out upon the broader stage of the nations? While the Church can point to innumerable testimonies of changed lives, there are also undeniable evidences of changed societies and nations through the influence of the Bible. For example, the late theologian B.B. Warfield had observed:

- Hospitals and asylums and refuges for the sick, the miserable and the afflicted grow like heaven-bedewed blossoms in its path. Woman, whose equality with man Plato considered a sure mark of social disorganization, has been elevated; slavery has been driven from civilized ground; literacy has been given by Christian missionaries, under the influence of the Bible.

If Warfield is correct, how does such a finding prove that the Bible is a gift from God? The Bible challenges us to "taste and see" (*Psalm 34:8*). If following the teachings of the Bible proves disastrous, it has failed this test. If it proves fruitful, it validates the Bible's claims. The entire Old Testament serves to demonstrate that when Israel followed God's Word, they were blessed in very tangible ways. When they turned away from His Word, they suffered, as Moses had repeatedly prophesied (*Deuteronomy 28, 29*).

Is this what we observe? Yes! Those nations – northern and Western Europe, North America, Australia…-- that had been nurtured by God's Word prospered. As they have rejected the Word, they have begun to slip, especially in comparison to the progress made by Eastern Asia.

The impact of the Christian missionaries has also borne witness to this principle. However, Western culture often associates missionaries with the imperialists, who had wanted to stamp out native cultures, and the colonialists who economically exploited them. However, new research has exposed the fallacies of these many stereotypes.

Robert Woodberry, professor of sociology, University of Texas, had devoted 14 years to investigate why certain countries had developed thriving democracies, while neighboring countries became failed states. Andrea Palpant Dilley writes that:

- Woodberry already had historical proof that missionaries had educated women and the poor, promoted widespread printing, let nationalistic movements that empowered ordinary citizens, and fueled other key elements of democracy. Now the statistics were backing it up: Missionaries weren't just part of the picture. They were *central* to it. (Dilly, 38)

To his amazement, Woodberry was discovering that a long denigrated ingredient – the missionary – was actually central to the creation of successful states. He writes:

- Areas where Protestant missionaries had a significant presence in the past are on average more economically developed today, with comparatively better health, lower infant mortality, lower corruption, greater literacy, higher educational attainment (especially for women), and more robust membership in non-governmental associations. (Dilley, 39)

- Pull out a map," says Woodberry, "point to any place where "conversionary Protestants" [evangelists] were active in the past, and you'll typically find more printed books and more schools per capita. You'll find too, that in Africa, the Middle East, and in parts of Asia, most of the early nationalists who led their countries to independence graduated from Protestant mission schools. (Dilley, 41)

Woodberry's thesis has been gaining support. Philip Jenkins, professor of history, Baylor University, claims:

- Try as I might to pick holes in it, the theory holds up.

Daniel Philpot, professor of political science and peace studies, Notre Dame, goes further:

- Why did some countries go democratic, while others went the route of theocracy or dictatorship…Conversionary Protestants are crucial to what makes the country democratic today…Not only is it another factor – it turns out to be the most important factor. It can't be anything but startling for scholars of democracy. (Dilley, 40)

Robin Grier, professor of economics, University of Oklahoma, confesses that although he is "not religious," "Bob's work…changed my views and caused me to rethink":

- I think it's the best work out there on religion and economic development… It's incredibly sophisticated and well-grounded. I haven't seen anything quite like it. (Dilley, 40)

Well, how about those missionaries that had collaborated with the imperialists?

Woodberry claims that these were the exceptions:

- We don't have to deny that there were and are racist missionaries… But if that were the average effect, we would expect the places where missionaries had influence to be worse than places where missionaries weren't allowed or were restricted in action. We find exactly the opposite on all kinds of outcomes. Even in places where few people converted, [missionaries] had a profound economic and political impact… One of the main stereotypes about missions is that they were closely connected to colonialism, but Protestant missionaries not funded by the state were regularly very critical of colonialism. (Dilley, 40)

It is noteworthy that it was only the Protestant missionaries who sought conversions that are associated with the growth of thriving democracies. Dilley writes:

- The positive effect of missionaries on democracy applies only to "conversionary Protestants." Protestant clergy financed by the state, as well as Catholic missionaries prior to the 1960s, had no comparable effect in the areas where they worked. (Dilley, 40)

Woodberry's conclusions have received support from other studies. Dilley writes:

- Over a dozen studies have confirmed Woodberry's findings. The growing body of research is beginning to change the way scholars, aid works, and economists think about democracy and development. (Dilley, 41)

In view of the above, the long disparaged missionary and even more so, the Word of God, deserve the recognition due them.

Christian missions and the impact of their Bible have gotten a bad rap. If you doubt this, just watch a *PBS* or a *BBC* history special on the subject. The missionaries who followed in the wake of the Conquistadores have received special condemnation. A *BBC* TV series of *The Missionaries* claims that,

- Under the guise of evangelism came harsh exploitation and eventually the enslavement of the Indians.

In "*6 Modern Myths about Christianity and Western Civilization,*" research fellow, Philip J. Sampson, attacks the myth that the missionaries were oppressors). Sampson counters that many of the missionaries had taken a strong stance against these colonial powers. He cites a sermon by

Dominican Antonio de Montesinos (1511), preached against the sins of the white colonists:

- Tell me, by what right and with what justice do you keep these poor Indians in such cruel and horrible servitude? By what authority have you made such detestable wars against these people…you kill them with your desire to extract and acquire gold every day…Are these not men…Are you not obliged to live them as you love yourselves?

Contrary to the philosophy of Aristotle who regarded the slave as a "live tool," the Bible grants dignity to all humanity as "created in the image of God (*Genesis 1:26*). Sampson points out the consequence of this:

- "Many 19th century missionaries were appalled at the slave trade and did their best to try to change it. William Burns opposed the 'coolie' trade in China and protested to British government representatives…Missionaries in East Africa were horrified at the local slave trade and were at a loss as to what to do about it. (Sampson, 100)

In her discussion of the missionaries to Africa, historian Ruth Tucker acknowledges that, while there were missionaries who also understood their role as one of westernizing the natives:

- They, more than any other outside influence, fought against the evils colonialism and imperialism brought. They waged long and bitter battles…the heinous traffic in human cargo. And after the demise of the slave trade they raised their voice against other crimes, including the bloody tactics King Leopold used to extract rubber from the Congo. The vast majority of missionaries were pro-African, and their stand for racial justice often made them despised by their European brothers. Indeed, it is no exaggeration to say that without the conscience of Christian missions, many of the crimes of colonialism would have gone entirely unchecked. (Tucker, 140).

Sampson explodes the myth that the missionaries were in collusion with the imperialists and colonists. In fact, the missionaries were often expelled by the colonial powers to prevent them from "publicizing atrocities or intervening to help the native people." (Sampson, 101) He agrees with Tucker that the:

- Missionaries in Africa were opposed to slavery from an early period, and they used a variety of means to oppose it, including buying slaves and establishing plantations for them to work on. (Sampson, 102)

According to Sampson, rather than collusion, conflict characterized missionary-colonialist relations:

- The missionaries insisted on treating native people as human beings who are entitled to the protection of the law, and this rubbed salt into the wound. It should come as no surprise, therefore, that colonists and traders often opposed missions. (Sampson, 103)

- Traders and colonists resisted the evangelism of native people, seeing conversion as the first step to indigenous people gaining access to the resources of Western culture and hence to the power that colonists wished to keep for themselves…Native people who wished to break free of the settler's stranglehold and worship God were immediately persecuted by the white traders. (Sampson, 103-104)

Stephen Neill's *"History of Christian Missions"* gives an example of this:

- The missionaries [to New Guinea] from the start found themselves in bitter opposition to the white traders and exploiters, whose attitude was expressed by one of them to John G. Patton in the words 'our watchword is 'Sweep these creatures away, and let the white men occupy the soil," and who, in pursuance of their aim, placed men sick of the measles on various islands in order to destroy the population through disease. (Neill, 355)

In contrast to the concerns of the missionaries, the educated, disdaining the idea of the "spiritual equality of all colors of Christians," aligned themselves with the exploiters:

- Missionaries, on the other hand, were ridiculed in scholarly journals for their shallow thinking in regard to race. (Tucker, 140)

Darwinism had made racism intellectually respectable. Evolutionist Karl Giberson, acknowledges the prevailing racism (Giberson):

- How shocking it is today to acknowledge that virtually every educated person in the Western culture at the time ...shared [evolutionist] Haeckel's [racist] ideas. Countless atrocities around the globe were rationalized by the belief that superior races were improving the planet by exterminating defective elements...there can be little doubt that such viewpoints muted voices that would otherwise have been raised in protest.

Consequently, evolutionists presented no rationale to oppose the abuses of colonialism. In contrast to this, Tucker cites A.F. Walls,

- But one thing is clear. If missions are associated with the rise of imperialism, they are equally associated with the factors which brought about its destruction." (Tucker, 111)

She also cites Ralph Winter:

- Protestant missionary efforts in this period led the way to establishing all around the world the democratic apparatus of government, the schools, the hospitals, the universities and the political foundations for the new nations. (Tucker, 111)

What greater testimony could there have been to the missionary dedication to those among whom they worked! Nevertheless, they have often been charged with the destruction of native culture. This is ironic because missions have done more to "codify and preserve [indigenous] languages" than has any other group:

- The anthropologist Mary Haas estimates that 'ninety per cent of the material available on American Indian languages, is missionary in origin. (Sampson, 109-110)

Indeed, the missionaries did campaign against certain native practices like female circumcision. Even Charles Darwin confessed:

- Human sacrifice…infanticide…bloody wars, where the conquerors spared neither women nor children—all these have been abolished…by the introduction of Christianity. (Sampson, 110)

Why then all the bad press against the missionary? Darwin proposed that:

- Disappointed in not finding the field of licentiousness quite so open as formerly, they [the Western traders] will not give credit to a morality which they do not wish to practice or to a religion which they undervalue, if not despise. (Sampson, 111)

Consequently, the historian Stephen Neill concludes that the:

- Weight of the evidence tells heavily against" the accusation that missionaries have been responsible for the destruction of native cultures. (Sampson, 111)

The Christian missionaries bravely opposed the prevailing worldview. Representative of the Darwinian thinking of his day, Richard F. Burton complained that the Christian willingness to treat Africans as "men and brethren" was "a dangerous error at odds with the evolutionary facts" (Sampson, 98). Instead, faith in the Gospel…

- Encouraged Dr. John Philip of the London Missionary Society to support native rights in South Africa in the early nineteenth century…Lancelot Threlkeld to demand equal protection under the law for the Awabakal people of Australia and also inspired John Eliot to persuade the Massachusetts courts to find in favor of native people against settler claims. Even so unsympathetic an author as David Stoll concedes that the contemporary missions in Latin America 'tended to treat native people with more respect than did national governments and fellow citizens.' (Sampson, 98)

This should be no surprise. It has been the faithfulness to their beliefs that has motivated Christians from the start. Regarding this, Philip Yancey provides some insights that he gleaned from the historian Rodney Stark:

- In the midst of a hostile environment, the Christians simply acted on their beliefs. Going against the majority culture, they treated slaves as human beings, often liberating them…When an epidemic hit their towns, they stayed behind to nurse the sick. They refused to participate in such common practices as abortion and infanticide. They responded to persecution as martyrs, not as terrorists. And when Roman social networks disintegrated, the church stepped in. Even one of their pagan critics had to acknowledge that early Christians loved their neighbors 'as if they were our own family.' (Yancey, 32-33) *Christianity Today*, Nov 2010, 32-33)

If a person can be judged by their fruits, then so too the Bible! The fruits of those who allowed the Bible to govern their lives are apparent, even if flawed in many ways. Even Western civilization points unmistakably to its sturdy biblical foundations.

Nevertheless, this shouldn't lead us to indiscriminately lump all religions and philosophies together. There are stark differences among them. Instead, it seems that wherever the Christian faith has trod, there have been positive outcomes. Former editor of the Sunday Telegraph, Dominic Lawson, in a review in the *Sunday Times* of Niall Ferguson's new book, *Civilisation: The West and the Rest*, carries a quote from a member of the *Chinese Academy of Social Sciences* in which he tries to account for the success of the West:

- We have realized that the heart of your culture is your religion: Christianity. That is why the West is so powerful. The Christian moral foundation of social and cultural life was what made possible the emergence of capitalism and then the successful transition to democratic politics. We don't have any doubt about this.

We would expect that a faith based upon a Book given by God should give evidence of its Author, although indirectly. Perhaps instead of the Bible being God-given, it is merely a collection of some useful, inspirational, and humane ideals. So let us continue on to examine proofs of a more objective nature.

WORKS CITED

Dilley, Andrea Palpant, "The Surprising Discovery About Those Colonialist, Proselytizing Missionaries," *Christianity Today*, "Jan/Feb 2014.

Giberson, Karl, *Saving Darwin: How to be a Christian and Believe in Evolution,* (HarperOne Reprint Edition, June 2, 2009)

Lawson, Dominic, *The Sunday Times Review of Niall Ferguson's new book, Civilisation: The West and the Rest,* Feb. 27, 2011
www.thetimes.co.uk/article

Neill, Stephen, *"History of Christian Missions", (*NYC: Penguin Books, 2nd Edition, 1991)

Sampson, Philip J., "*6 Modern Myths about Christianity and Western Civilization*," (InterVarsity Press, 2001)

Tucker, Ruth, *("From Jerusalem to Irian Jaya – A Biographical History of Christian Missions* (Grand Rapids: Zondervan, 2004)

Yancey, Philip, "A Living Stream in the Desert: How the Christian Faith Will be a Subversive and Liberating Influence in the Middle East," *Christianity Today*, (Nov 2010, 32-33)

Chapter 6

THE TORAH: GOD'S WORD

The last two chapters only provided indirect or suggestive evidence that the Bible is the Word of God. I continued to struggle with the gnawing doubt that perhaps the benefits associated with the Bible could be explained another way, without requiring God? Therefore, the following chapters will focus on the direct evidence of the Scriptures. In this chapter, I want to argue that the Torah couldn't have been the invention of men. Why not? It doesn't reflect the interests or perspectives of men but of God.

I have written the following essay on the subject which has been published in the *Christian Research Journal*:

In contrast, the *Wellhausen Hypothesis* (The Documentary Hypothesis - DH) had asserted that the Old Testament (OT), especially the Torah, is nothing more than the product of numerous editors who cut and pasted the OT together from a shabby assortment of previously existing documents in order to suit their political agendas. Here's how Wikipedia describes it:

- The documentary hypothesis...proposes that the Pentateuch (the first five books of the Bible) was derived from originally independent, parallel and complete narratives, which were subsequently combined into the current form by a series of redactors [editors]. (www.wikipedia.org, Documentary Hypothesis)

Many have ably critiqued the DH. The late OT scholar, Gleason Archer, concluded:

- The *Wellhausen Hypothesis* was allegedly based upon the evidence of the text itself, and yet the evidence of the text is consistently evaded whenever it happens to go counter to the theory. (Archer, 110)

However, there are other ways to debunk the DH. One way argues that the OT reflects a Divine agenda rather than a human one, as claimed by the DH. Here are just a very limited number of evidences that we might consider:

Instead of giving the Israelites a sense of superiority, Moses (and the Prophets) consistently revealed how utterly unworthy they were of anything from God:

- It is not because of your righteousness or your integrity that you are going in to take possession of their land; but on account of the wickedness of these nations, the LORD your God will drive them out before you, to accomplish what he swore to your fathers, to Abraham, Isaac and Jacob. Understand, then, that it is not because of your righteousness that the LORD your God is giving you this good land to possess, for you are a stiff-necked people. (*Deuteronomy 9:5-6*).

Israel wasn't chosen by God because they were superior. Instead, they were a stubborn, "stiff-necked" people. No nation, trying to convince its people that they were worthy (and this is what people want), would ever try to portray themselves this way. Why should Israel accept such a disparaging revelation unless the hand of God had been so manifestly present!

In contrast to this disparaging picture, religions use marketplace strategies to lend appeal to their products. Orthodox Jewish writer, David Klinghoffer, concludes that Jewish rejection of Jesus is founded in "the mystic uniqueness of the Jewish essence or nature. There was something distinct about the Jewish soul…The Jewish soul feels the worlds, in a remarkably visceral way, as unredeemed."

He bases this opinion upon Judah Loeb's famous interpretation of the Talmud tractate, Avodah Zarah, which stated that God had offered the Torah to all the other nations first, "to see if they possessed a predisposition to the Torah, and did not find it in them," in contrast to what God found in the Jews. (Klinghoffer, 215-217)

This type of chauvinism (the aggrandizement of one's own people) is found in all religions. For instance, the Koran reads:

- You are the best nation ever brought forth to men, bidding to honour, and forbidding dishonour, and believing in Allah. (*Surah 3:110-112*)

- The unbelievers of the People of the Book and the idolaters shall be in the Fire of Gehenna, therein dwelling forever; those are the worst of creatures. (*Surah 98:6*)

Why is the OT, specifically the Torah, so different in this regards? Perhaps because it confronts us with a Divine perspective, rather than a human agenda!

Moses prophesied Israel's inevitable failures and sufferings:

- But to this day the LORD has not given you a mind that understands or eyes that see or ears that hear. (*Deuteronomy 29:4; 30:6*)

- He [Israel] abandoned the God who made him and rejected the Rock his Savior. They made him jealous with their foreign gods and angered him with their detestable idols. They sacrificed to demons, which are not God...You deserted the Rock, who fathered you; you forgot the God who gave you birth. The LORD saw this and rejected them...they are a perverse generation, children who are unfaithful. (*Deuteronomy 32:15-19*)

No one would invent such a religion! Whenever we try to sell a product, we assure the buyer that they will profit from it. Instead, Moses assured the people that they would fail and suffer because of this religion.

Why then did Israel persevere with this humanly offensive faith? Why did they acknowledge such books as canonical? Only because God had made His presence surpassingly tangible to Israel! They had been deprived of any reason to deny that the books of the Bible came from Him.

Religions not only aggrandize their particular followers, they also prophesy *only* **their future blessedness.** However, the Torah (and especially the Prophets) mentions the eventual blessedness of the Gentiles (the other nations). God gave Moses a song to teach to Israel, covering both their past and future. It concludes this way:

- Rejoice, O nations, with his people, for he will avenge the blood of his servants; he will take vengeance on his enemies and make atonement for his land and people. (*Deuteronomy 32:43*)

Our Patriarchal forefathers, Abraham, Isaac, and Jacob, are portrayed as scoundrels, pimps, cheats and liars—not the heroes that the Jewish commentaries portray them to be. For instance:

- The Kuzari (Rabbi Judah HaLevi, 1075-1141) states that Abraham was gifted with high intelligence; and, as Maimonides (1135-1204) describes, Abraham didn't blindly accept the ubiquitous idolatry. The whole populace had been duped, but the young Abraham contemplated the matter relentlessly, finally arriving at the conclusion that there is One God. (www.wiki.answers.com)

However, these rabbis have absolutely no Biblical or historical justification for their claims, just their own fanciful speculations. Unsurprisingly, God chose Abraham because he was more deserving—more virtuous than others, from a Jewish perspective:

- Abram tried to convince his father, Terach, of the folly of idol worship. One day, when Abram was left alone to mind the store, he took a hammer and smashed all of the idols except the largest one. He placed the hammer in the hand of the largest idol. When his father returned and asked what happened, Abram said, "The idols got into a fight, and the big one smashed all the other ones." His father said, "Don't be ridiculous. These idols have no life or power. They can't do anything." Abram replied, "Then why do you worship them?" (www.jewfaq.org/)

- Abraham nomadically wandered the length and breadth of the land proclaiming his belief, and he was so successful that he converted thousands to monotheism. His method was one of kindness—he set up a motel and after feeding and watering wayfarers they were introduced to the true belief and blessed G-d the Provider. Abraham converted the men and Sarah the women, and together they successfully brought many souls under the wings of the Shechinah, hence resensitizing the world to G-dliness. (www.chabad.org)

These legends reflect our human tendency to aggrandize our forefathers. However, according the Genesis account, there was very little appealing about them. They are hardly the role-models that we'd invent in order to make our religion appealing to perspective buyers. Instead, we find that there is only one Role-Model.

Jacob, who was later named "Israel" through his baffling encounter with God, became the namesake of the Israelite nation. However, according to the Genesis account, he was far less than virtuous. He not only connived his brother Esau out of his birthright (*Genesis 25:29-34*), he also deceived his father into giving him the blessing Isaac had intended for Esau! (*Genesis 27*)

The other Israelite heroes are similarly tarnished. The patriarch Judah, the namesake of the Jewish people, visited prostitutes and had intercourse with his daughter-in-law. Moses, arguably the greatest Israelite, was even portrayed as a sinner who was unworthy to enter the Promised Land (*Deuteronomy 34*).

The future monarchy, rather than being presented as God's ideal, appears to be God's reluctant concession to His stubborn people. The kings are warned that they are no better or more deserving than others and are subject to the same laws (*Deuteronomy 17:19-20*). This legislation does not reflect the interests of the monarchy or ruling class, whose interest it would have been to promote a strong and unassailable monarchy possessing the divine rights of Kingship.

The laws protecting the poor and marginalized could not have been the product of the rich and privileged. The poor could glean grapes and grain from the vineyards of the rich (*Deuteronomy 24:24-25*). Such a law could not protect the interests of the rich and powerful who characteristically make such laws to protect their own interests. Instead, we are hard-pressed to understand the Mosaic Laws as humanly derived.

Wellhausen, on the other hand, postulated that the Israelite religion had been the product of the rich and powerful. However, so many of its laws fail to reflect this self-serving perspective. For instance, the Sabbath Year specified, "At the end of every seven years you must cancel debts." (*Deuteronomy 15:1-2*).

Such a law could not favor the rich and powerful! What then could explain its source, if not God!

Slaves had to be freed:

- If a fellow Hebrew, a man or a woman, sells himself to you and serves you six years, in the seventh year you must let him go free. (*Deuteronomy 15:12*)

This too would not coincide with the interests of the rich and powerful, the alleged authors of the Bible. Nor would the institution of a Sabbath Day, which gave rest to both slaves and animals, be the invention of the educated writers.

The Jubilee took the land from the rich and powerful, returning this original inheritance to the poor (*Leviticus 25:13*). Such a law went against prevailing interests to such a degree that we don't have any evidence that it was ever followed!

Whenever soldiers feared for their safety, the law encouraged them to go AWOL – hardly the legislation of a ruling class wanting to protect its interests:

- Then the officers shall add, "Is any man afraid or fainthearted? Let him go home…"(*Deuteronomy 20:8*)

The Levites were not legally entitled to any inheritance of land. Land was wealth! Why would the priestly caste ever institute or allow such legislation unless it came from above!

The ordained holidays do not commemorate any historical event (the Passover is the one clear exception) but instead are almost entirely lacking in historical content. However, nations do not establish undefined holidays. No one would embrace them!

For instance, the purpose for the "Feast of Trumpets" was never specified. Therefore, the Rabbis invented a meaning for it. They called the day, "Rosh Hashanah" (the head of the year) or "New Years Day." How strange not to know the significance of one's holidays! Had they been humanly ordained, there never would have been any question!

Holidays commemorate past events. Characteristically, all of Israel's non-divinely-ordained holidays are commemorative. Hanukkah commemorates the cleansing of the Temple and the Maccabean military victories. Purim commemorates the salvation of the Jewish people in Persia. T'sha b'Av commemorates the destruction of the Temple. Simchat Torah commemorates the giving of the Law on Sinai.

Similarly, we assign dates to occasions we want to remember – dates that serve to define us as a nation. Not so the Torah! There is no assignment of a date to the giving of the law, to any military victories or momentous defeats (like Pearl Harbor Day). There is no "Victory over Jericho" day or "Pharaoh's Defeat in the Red Sea" day. Instead, it seems that these dates are important to God, perhaps even prophetic.

The Law placed everyone under the curse of death:

- Cursed is the man who does not uphold the words of this law by carrying them out. (*Deuteronomy 27:26*)

Ordinarily, we would not accept such a damning religion. Nor would the Rabbis, who qualified this teaching in several ways! For instance, Rabbi Gerald Sigal wrote (Sigal, pg):

- [*Deuteronomy 27:26*] does not refer to the breaking of the Law by an ordinary individual. It is, as the Rabbis explain, a reference to the authorities in power who fail to enforce the rule of the Law in the land of Israel (*Talmud – J.T. Sotah 7:4*). The leadership of the nation is thus charged, under pain of the curse, to set the tone for the nation and make the Law the operative force in the life of the nation.

Instead, this verse damns every Israelite, as do so many other verses (*Exodus 20:6; 23:21-22; 24:3; Leviticus 26:14-16; Deuteronomy 5:29; 6:24-25; 8:1; 10:12; 11:8, 26-28, 32; 12:28*). For this reason, the Psalms repeatedly inform Israel that their only hope was in the mercy of God (*Psalm 143:2; 32:1-5; 130:3-8*)!

Consistent with this, there is no verse in the OT that applauds Israel in such a manner: "You Israelites are doing a great job! Keep up the good work!" Instead, the OT is consistently degrading.

Humanly speaking, the Torah's teaching is so humanly degrading and so counter to our interests that anyone who wanted to gain a following would never invent such a religion! Instead, we humans tend to come to religion for its benefits and not its curses!

Meanwhile, the DH ascribes the OT to human devices and self-serving manipulations. However, we find the very opposite in the pages of the OT – a religion that humans would not invent! Instead, it appears that we are looking at a Divinely-given Book – the very thing that it has always insisted upon!

WORKS CITED

Archer, Gleason, *Survey of Old Testament Introductions,* (Chicago: Moody Press, 1964)

Klinghoffer, David, *Why the Jews Rejected Jesus,* (New York: Doubleday, First Edition, 2005)

Sigal, Gerald, *The Jew and the Christian Missionary,* (NYC: KTAV Publishing House, 1981)

www.chabad.org/library/article_cdo/aid/361874/jewish/Abraham.htm

www.en.wikipedia.org/wiki/Documentary_hypothesis

www.jewfaq.org/origins.htm

www.wiki.answers.com/

Chapter 7

THE JEWS: THE SIGN-PEOPLE OF GOD

Fulfilled prophecy also points to the fact that the Bible is God's Word. The Jews are the sign-people of God, showing forth both God's mercy and wrath because of their rejection of their God.

A certain Russian Czar demanded that his advisor, "Prove that there is a God!" The advisor answered, "Just look at the Jewish people!"

What did he mean by this? The Hebrew Bible's prophecies about this wandering nation have been unusual and fulfilled in dramatic ways. Moses declared that God had chosen Israel and had blessed them exceedingly but also prophesied:

- You may say to yourself, "My power and the strength of my hands have produced this wealth for me." But remember the LORD your God, for it is he who gives you the ability to produce wealth, and so confirms his covenant, which he swore to your forefathers, as it is today. If you ever forget the LORD your God and follow other gods and worship and bow down to them, I testify against you today that you will surely be destroyed. (*Deuteronomy 8:17-19*)

Moses claimed that if Israel remained faithful to God's covenant, they would be blessed (*Deuteronomy 28*). Since that time, no people has ever been as successful, learned, and wealthy as the Jewish people. Achievement has followed them wherever Israel had been exiled. Their degrading exilic circumstances (which have destroyed other peoples) had not interfered with God's blessings to His sign people. He has always brought forth His broken and persecuted people

77

against all the odds and the hatred of the surrounding peoples.

Hank Pellissier has documented some of the successes of this incredible sign-people of God (Pellissier, www.ieet.org):

- **Nobel Prizes**: "Since 1950, 29% of the awards have gone to Ashkenazim [the Yiddish speaking Jews from northern Europe, even though they represent only 0.25% of humanity. Ashkenazi achievement in this arena is 117 times greater than their population."

- **Hungary in the 1930s**: "Ashkenazim were 6% of the population, but they comprised 55.7% of physicians, 49.2% of attorneys, 30.4% of engineers, and 59.4% of bank officers; plus, they owned 49.4% of the metallurgy industry, 41.6% of machine manufacturing, 72.8% of clothing manufacturing, and, as housing owners, they received 45.1% of Budapest rental income. Jews were similarly successful in nearby nations, like Poland and Germany."

- **USA** (today): "Ashkenazi Jews comprise 2.2% of the USA population, but they represent 30% of faculty at elite colleges, 21% of Ivy League students, 25% of the Turing Award winners, 23% of the wealthiest Americans, and 38% of the Oscar-winning film directors."

However, there have also been the opposite extremes. Moses prophesied that Israel would reject their God and He would reject them, resulting in terrifying consequence (*Deuteronomy 32*):

- The LORD will drive you and the king you set over you to a nation unknown to you or your fathers. There you will worship other gods, gods of wood and stone. You will become a thing of horror and an object of scorn and ridicule to all the nations where the LORD will drive you...Among those nations you will find no repose, no resting place for the sole of your foot. There the LORD will give you an anxious mind, eyes weary with longing, and a despairing heart. You will live in constant suspense, filled with dread both night and day, never sure of your life. (*Deuteronomy 28:36-37; 65-66*)

There has never been a people as hated and persecuted as the Jewish people. Yet, from the midst of this hatred, their God had promised restoration to exiled and tormented Israel:

- But if they will confess their sins and the sins of their fathers--their treachery against me and their hostility toward me, which made me hostile toward them so that I sent them into the land of their enemies--then when their uncircumcised hearts are humbled and they pay for their sin, I will remember my covenant with Jacob and my covenant with Isaac and my covenant with Abraham, and I will remember [My promise about the] land. (*Leviticus 26:40-42*)

On three occasions, God had rescued His broken and once again repentant people, brought them back to the land, and re-established their nation:

1. In response to the cries of enslaved Israel's cries, after hundreds of years of cruel bondage in Egypt, God sent Moses to lead them to redemption and freedom in the Promised Land.

2. After the fall of the Babylonian empire in 532 BC, God placed it in the Persian Cyrus' heart to equip the Jews to return to their own land and rebuild their Temple.

3. Following the two rebellions against Rome (66-70 CE and 132-136 CE), the Jews were expelled from their land. After centuries of persecution culminating in the Holocaust in Nazi Europe, once again, Israel was restored as a nation by the 1948 UN vote.

No people group has ever returned to its ancestral land—-even once—after entirely leaving it. Israel has been restored to their Promised Land on three occasions! This is not merely an historical anomaly; it is a sign of Divine intervention.

However, even today we find that Israel has once again turned from their God. Even the Orthodox Jews pay scant attention to the Hebrew Scriptures (*Tenach*) and have instead favored the writings of their rabbis. When they do invoke these Scriptures, it is through rabbinic eyes, which insist on rejecting the clear and direct meanings in favor of the "hidden" ones, thereby side-stepping of Words of God.

Meanwhile, we observe anti-Semitism and anti-Israel resolutions escalating at alarming rates, while the Jewish people once again fail to read the signs that have been prophesied repeatedly (*Deuteronomy 32:28-29; Isaiah 6:9-10*). After the Holocaust, they vowed, "Never again!" However, the rejection of their God has hardened them against both God and the impending dangers, even to the point of allying themselves to those who seek their utter destruction.

However, prophecy reveals that, in the end, Israel will once again be a nation and once again a nation without faith towards her God. Her assailants will mercilessly break her, but this time her God will intervene decisively and permanently:

- The LORD will judge ["vindicate" ESV] his people and have compassion on his servants when he sees their strength is gone and no one is left, slave or free…Rejoice, O nations, with his people, for he will avenge the blood of his servants; he will take vengeance on his enemies and make atonement for his land and people. (*Deuteronomy 32:36; 43*)

Their God will also open Israel's eyes to the One whom they had rejected:

- And I will pour out on the house of David and the inhabitants of Jerusalem a spirit of grace and pleas for mercy, so that, when they look on me, on him whom they have pierced, they shall mourn for him, as one mourns for an only child, and weep bitterly over him, as one weeps over a firstborn. (*Zechariah 12:10; Jeremiah 50:4; Revelation 1:7*)

Fulfilled prophecy about this sign-people of God not only constitutes proof of God's existence; it also validates Scripture and even the Christian faith.

WORKS CITED

Pellisinger, Hank,
www.ieet.org/index.php/IEET2/more/pellissier20110719

Chapter 8

THE MIRACLES OF JESUS

Was Jesus a miracle worker? If not, then why believe Him! This too was exactly His reasoning:

- "If I am not doing the works of my Father, then do not believe me; but if I do them, even though you do not believe me, believe the works, that you may know and understand that the Father is in me and I am in the Father." (*John 10:37-38*)

If Jesus had routinely been performing miracles, it strongly suggests that He was doing them by the hand of God to authenticate His teachings. Therefore, His contemporaries should have had every reason in the world to believe in Him, even though they refused.

But why should we believe? For one thing, many of us have experienced the authenticating miracles of God. For another, the historical evidence in favor of this is so overwhelming that even the skeptics of the *Jesus Seminar* had acknowledged that He had been performing miracles. Here is a small sampling of their opinions:

- On historical grounds it is virtually indisputable that Jesus was a healer and exorcist. (Marcus Borg, *Jesus a New Vision: Spirit*), (Bishop, www.reasonsforjesus.com/6-reasons-takes-faith-to-deny-jesus/)

- Jesus was both an exorcist and a healer. (John Crossan, *"The Historical Jesus: The Life of a Mediterranean Jewish Peasant"*), (Bishop, www.reasonsforjesus.com/58-scholar-quote-jesus-miracles/)

-

Based on the historical evidence, many other unbelieving scholars also acknowledged that Jesus was a miracle worker:

- An ability to work cures, further, coheres with another datum from Jesus' mission: He had a popular following, which such an ability helps to account for. (Paula Fredriksen, *"Jesus of Nazareth, King of the Jews"*), (Bishop, ibid.)

- [W]e note that Jesus as exorcist, healer (even to the point of raising the dead), and miracle worker is one of the strongest, most ubiquitous, and most variously attested depictions in the Gospels. All strata of this material—Mark, John, M-traditions, L-traditions, and Q—make this claim. This sort of independent multiple attestation supports arguments for the antiquity of a given tradition, implying that its source must lie prior to its later, manifold expressions, perhaps in the mission of Jesus himself. (Paula Fredriksen, *"Jesus of Nazareth, King of the Jews"*) (Bishop, ibid.)

- Whatever you think about the philosophical possibility of miracles of healing, it's clear that Jesus was widely reputed to have done them. ." (Bart Ehrman, *"The New Testament: A Historical Introduction to the Early Christian Writings"*) (Bishop, ibid.)

- Most of the miracle stories contained in the gospels are legendary or at least are dressed up with legends. But there can be no doubt that Jesus did such deeds, which were, in his and his contemporaries' understanding, miracles, that is, deeds that were the result of supernatural, divine causality. Doubtless he healed the sick and cast out demons. (Rudolf Bultmann, *'Jesus'*), (Bishop, ibid.)

In light of the above, Christian scholars have concluded:

- Even the most skeptical critics cannot deny that the historical Jesus carried out a ministry of miracle-working and exorcism. (Craig; *"The Evidence for Jesus", www.reasonablefaith.org)*

- Most historical Jesus scholars today, regardless of their personal theological orientation, do accept that Jesus drew crowds who believed that he performed cures and exorcisms. (Craig Keener; *"The Gospels as Sources for Historical Information about Jesus"*), (Bishop, www.reasonsforjesus.com/6-reasons-takes-faith-to-deny-jesus/)

- It is noteworthy that Jesus' enemies are not presented as denying that he did extraordinary deeds; rather they attributed them to evil origins, either to the devil *(Mark 3:22-30)* or in the 2d-century polemic to magic (Irenaeus, *'Against Heresies,' 2.32.3-5).*" (Raymond Brown; *"An Introduction to New Testament Christology."*), (Bishop, www.reasonsforjesus.com/58-scholar-quote-jesus-miracles/

- Brown's reflections are particularly true of the ancient Jewish writings, which reluctantly acknowledge Jesus' miracles. Here are some references from the Talmud, a compilation (Cir. 550 AD) of earlier Rabbinic writings, where Jesus is often pejoratively called "Jesu" instead of "Jesus." The Talmud dismissively refers to his miracles as "magic" or "sorcery," products of Satan. However, these pejorative terms also acknowledge that Jesus had been performing miracles:

- On Passover Eve they hanged Jesus of Nazareth. He practiced sorcery, incited and led Israel astray...Was Jesus of Nazareth deserving of a search for an argument in his favor? He was an enticer and the Torah says, 'You shall not spare, nor shall you conceal him! (*Sanhedrin 43A*)

- Jesus was a magician and a fool. Mary was an adulteress. (*Shabbath 104b*).

- Jesus... stood up a brick to symbolize an idol and bowed down to it. Jesus performed magic and incited the people of Israel and led them astray. (*Sanhedrin 107B*)

Celsus, writing against the Christian faith, 150-170 AD, confirms that the Talmudic assertions are about Jesus:

- Let us imagine what a Jew - let alone a philosopher - might say to Jesus: 'Is it not true, good sir, that you fabricated the story of your birth from a virgin to quiet rumors about the true and unsavory circumstances of your origins? Is it not the case that far from being born in the royal David's city of Bethlehem, you were born in a poor country town, and of a woman who earned her living by spinning? Is it not the case that when her deceit was uncovered, to wit, that she was pregnant by a roman soldier called Panthera [as in *Shabbath 104b*] she was driven away by her husband- the carpenter- and convicted of adultery?

How do modern rabbinic authorities regard this evidence? According to *The Jewish Encyclopedia*, Jesus was often accused by the Talmudists of performing magic:

- It is the tendency of all these sources to belittle the person of Jesus by ascribing to him illegitimate birth, magic, and a shameful death …

- Magic may have been ascribed him over against the miracles recorded in the Gospels …

- The sojourn of Jesus in Egypt is an essential part of the story of his youth. According to the Gospels he was in that country in his early infancy, but Celsus says that he was in service there and learned magic …

  o According to Celsus (in Origen, "Contra Celsum," i. 28) and to the Talmud (SHabakkuk 104b), Jesus learned magic in Egypt and performed his miracles by means of it; the latter work, in addition, states that he cut the magic formulas into his skin. It does not mention, however, the nature of his magic performances (Tosef., SHabakkuk xi. 4; Yer. SHabakkuk 18d); but as it states that the disciples of Jesus healed the sick "in the name of Jesus Pandera" (Yer. SHabakkuk 14d; Ab. Zarah 27b; Eccl. R. i. 8) it may be assumed that its author held the miracles of Jesus also to have been miraculous cures. Different in nature is the witchcraft attributed to Jesus in the "Toledot." When Jesus was expelled from the circle of scholars, he is said to have returned secretly from Galilee to Jerusalem, where he inserted a parchment containing the "declared name of God" ("Shem ha-Meforash"), which was guarded in the Temple, into his skin, carried it away, and then, taking it out of his skin, he performed his miracles by its means. This magic formula then had to be recovered from him, and Judah the Gardener (a personage of the "Toledot" corresponding to Judas Iscariot) offered to do it; he and Jesus then engaged in an aerial battle (borrowed from the legend of SIMON MAGUS), in which Judah remained victor and Jesus fled.

- The accusation of magic is frequently brought against Jesus. Jerome mentions it, quoting the Jews: "Magum vocant et Judaei Dominum meum" ("Ep. 1v., ad Ascellam," i. 196, ed. Vallarsi); Marcus, of the sect of the Valentinians, was, according to Jerome, a native of Egypt, and was accused of being, like Jesus, a magician (Hilgenfeld, 870). The accusation of magic is frequently brought against Jesus … As Balaam the magician and, according to the derivation of his name, "destroyer of the people", was from both of these points of view a good prototype of Jesus, the latter was also called "Balaam."

- Jesus performed all his miracles by means of magic (*The Jewish Encyclopedia*, (www.come-and-hear.com/editor/censorship_2.html)

Jewish historian Josephus (90 AD) also attested to Jesus' miracles. However, without any hard evidence, most scholars regard all or part of this as an interpolation (a later addition or emendation):

- About this time arose Jesus, a wise man, who did good deeds and whose virtues were recognized. And many Jews and people of other nations became his disciples. Pilate condemned him to be crucified and to die. However, those who became his disciples preached his doctrine. They related that he had appeared to them three days after his crucifixion and that he was alive. Perhaps he was the Messiah in connection with whom the prophets foretold wonders. (Josephus, XVIII 3.2)

In summary, even the skeptics and those who had only contempt for Jesus have acknowledged His miracles. Even though they do not regard these miracles as attesting to the fact that Jesus is the promised Messiah, this is where the evidence points. Besides, if Jesus is who He claimed to be, we are coerced by the evidence to accept His testimony about Scripture:

- But he answered [the devil], "It is written, 'Man shall not live by bread alone, but by <u>every word</u> that comes from the mouth of God.' (*Matthew 4:4*)

Jesus believed that every Word of Scripture came from God (*Matthew 5:16-19*). If we are to call ourselves followers of Jesus, we also must receive Scripture as Jesus did.

The insistence upon "every Word" wasn't an appeal to blind faith. Instead, Jesus taught His disciples to even be skeptical of even His claims. In accordance with the Hebrew Scriptures (*Deuteronomy 19:15*), Jesus taught that everything had to be confirmed by evidence and not blind faith. He even applied this principle to Himself:

- If I alone bear witness about myself, my testimony is not true. There is another who bears witness about me, and I know that the testimony that he bears about me is true. You sent to John, and he has borne witness to the truth…But the testimony that I have is greater than that of John. For the works that the Father has given me to accomplish, the very works that I am doing bear witness about me that the Father has sent me. And the Father who sent me has himself borne witness about me. (*John 5:31-37; 10:37-38*)

The writings of the Apostles remained true to this principle. They did not resort to deceptive means to fan up the faith of their flock. They understood that simply providing the evidence of the historical Jesus would suffice (*John 20:31*).

The miracles of Jesus validate His message, and His message affirmed the divinity of the Hebrew Scriptures. The resurrection, which we will later examine, also validates His message. However, can we believe the Gospel accounts? This will be our focus in the next chapter.

WORKS CITED

Bishop, James, (3/20/17*), "6 Reasons Why It Takes Faith to Deny Jesus",*
www.reasonsforjesus.com/6-reasons-takes-faith-to-deny-jesus/)

Bishop, James, (10/7/16), *"58 Scholar Quotes on Jesus' Miracles",*
www.reasonsforjesus.com/58-scholar-quote-jesus-miracles/

Craig, William, Lane, *The Evidence for Jesus*,
www.reasonablefaith.org

The Jewish Encyclopedia,
www.come-and-hear.com/editor/censorship_2.html

Josephus, *Jewish Antiquities*, XVIII 3.2)

Chapter 9

THE AUTHENTICITY OF THE FOUR GOSPELS

Can we trust the four canonical Gospels – Matthew, Mark, Luke and John? Are the teachings they ascribe to Jesus authentic? The Jesus Seminar (JS), a collection of skeptical Bible critics active in the 1980s and 90s concluded that only 18% the sayings that the Gospels had attributed to Jesus were His.

For many, this puts the kibosh on the Bible. If it's not authentic, then it can no longer be regarded as the Word of God. However, many gifted NT scholars have subsequently addressed the methodological fallacies and erroneous presuppositions that had given rise to the JS conclusions.

On a positive note, there are many reasons why we *should* regard the Gospels as authentic, such as:

1. The Miracles of Jesus
2. Fulfilled Prophecy
3. Internal Consistency
4. External Confirmation
5. The Wisdom of the Writings
6. Personal Transformation

I'd like to focus on one additional way. Jesus teachings, as found in the four Gospel accounts, could not represent human embellishments or inventions. Humans (Christians) would not invent such teachings and events! Why not? Jesus' words are offensive, confusing and even seem to contradict the interests and teachings of the early church. When we examine the Jesus of the Gospels, we find that virtually *everything* He did and said cut against the grain of not only His contemporaries, but also His Apostles and even the Early Church.

THE ASSOCIATES OF JESUS

Christ's 12 chosen apostles were all simple men. They weren't highly educated – not at all the type of people with whom educated elites or even the Early Church would want to identify; certainly not the type of people who would draw new converts.

Even worse, Jesus' 12 are *consistently* portrayed as simpletons who just didn't get it. Nowhere in the Gospels do we find Jesus telling them that they had done a good job or that they were catching on. On one occasion, Jesus did affirm Peter's response, but then followed it with a stinging denunciation:

- Get behind me, Satan! You are a stumbling block to me; you do not have in mind the things of God, but the things of men. (*Matthew 16:23*)

In fact the Apostles misunderstood almost all of Christ's teachings. Even at the end, the Apostles seemed to be so filled with themselves that they refused to believe what Jesus told them:

- You will all fall away," Jesus told them, for it is written: 'I will strike the shepherd, and the sheep will be scattered.' (*Mark 14:27*)

However, each of the Apostles confidently protested that he would never abandon Jesus. Later, they had to eat their words. As a matter of fact, Christ's absolute inner circle of disciples could not even stay awake to pray with their Master, as He had requested them to do.

If the early church had invented the four Gospels, the writers of such a "fiction" would have presented a glowing and winsome portrait of the Apostles.   After all, those same

Apostles would become the foundation and exponents of the movement. A glowing report would lend status to this new and embattled religion. However, we find no indication of this kind of window-dressing. Instead, the apostles are *consistently* presented as morally bankrupt, status-conscious and even racist. They looked up to everyone socially above them and tried to place impediments in front of those petitioners they regarded as inferior. At times, the Apostles physically blocked the blind, children and Gentiles from coming to Jesus. Meanwhile, they held the rich and powerful in high regard. (*Matthew 19:25*)

Who would want anything to do with such characters, and who would invent such patriarchs if they wanted their religion to flourish? No one! Why then do we have such consistently disparaging portrayals of the Apostles in the Gospels? The answer is simple—the accounts are true! The New Testament writers were more concerned about the accuracy of what they wrote than how attractive they could make their story sound.

There is something else we need to remember here. Jesus received the worst of sinners into His presence. Consequently, the ruling class concluded that He couldn't possibly be a prophet. How could He be, if He allowed degraded women to touch Him? (*Luke 7:39*)

And it wasn't only the ruling class which felt this way. The entire culture partook of this worldview, but He reserved His strongest denunciations for those who were the most highly respected. This is certainly not something you would do if you were starting a religion and wanted endorsements!

How then could such a Man have a following? He must have been a miracle-worker. Many of the skeptics associated with the *Jesus Seminar* have reluctantly admitted as much:

1. On historical grounds it is virtually indisputable that Jesus was a healer and exorcist. (Markus Borg, *"The Mighty Deeds of Jesus"*), (Bishop, www.reasonsforjesus.com/58-scholar-quote-jesus-miracles/)

2. Throughout his life, Jesus performed healings and exorcisms for ordinary people. (John Domonic Crossan, *"The Historical Jesus: The Life of a Mediterranean Jewish Peasant"*, (Bishop, ibid.)

3. On the eve of the Passover Yesu was hanged…because he practiced sorcery and led Israel astray. (Babylonian Talmud; Jewish sources have an aversion against mentioning Jesus by name and anything positive about Him.)

4. Jesus certainly performed exorcisms as they were practiced in the first century…It would have been natural for an itinerant charismatic healer and teacher to do so. (John Jacques Rousseau)

THE EVENTS OF JESUS' LIFE

Jesus was baptized by John the Baptist. It makes it seem that He had a sin to confess. No one would have invented such an account. The fact that He was tempted by the Devil for 40 days suggests that He could be tempted. This would seem to be inconsistent with the Early Church's alleged agenda to prove that Jesus is God.

We also see a Jesus confessing ignorance about His return: "Not even the son of man knows" (*Mark 13:32*). The Gospel accounts of Jesus in the Garden of Gethsemane reveal a fearful and reluctant Jesus. On the Cross, we see a "confused" Jesus, crying out to His Father, "Why have You forsaken Me?" – Hardly the portrait of Jesus that the Early

Church would want to convey, if they wanted to prove that Jesus is the promised Messiah!

In contrast to the Gospels, every other religion paints their leader departing in style, as an inspiration and an example for all the followers. However, Jesus departed in utter disgrace – beaten, stripped naked, murdered as a common criminal, abandoned by His Apostles. This is not a portrait that others would find inspiring. Why should the Gospels include these embarrassing accounts unless they *actually* happened this way? Besides, the thousands that had come to faith in Jerusalem after the Crucifixion must have been convinced that this wasn't the end of the story.

Why were the women, whose testimony lacked any credibility in that culture, acknowledged as the first ones to encounter the risen Lord? Again, it must have happened that way! No! Christian would have invented such an account.

JESUS' TEACHINGS

Some of Jesus' teachings were difficult to understand. Others were impossible to follow and would discourage would-be followers. On one occasion, Jesus taught:

- I tell you the truth, unless you eat the flesh of the Son of Man and drink his blood, you have no life in you. (*John 6:53*)

As a result of this difficult teaching, many departed from Him. However, just about all of His teachings were difficult to understand. He taught, "Hate mother and father," "Let the dead bury the dead," "Cut off hands," "Don't let your left hand know what your right is doing."

His Parables were no less challenging. None of them had appeal to the common man or the leadership. Most were highly offensive. None would warm the heart, except perhaps for the *Parable of the Prodigal Son*. But even this parable afflicts those who think that they are righteous.

Almost all of His Parables criticize cherished religious assumptions. The account of *The Rich Young Man* teaches that humanity is incapable of salvation (*Matthew 19:26*). *The Workers in the Vineyard* (*Matthew 20:1-16*) insultingly teaches that many of those who had worked the longest and the hardest in the Lord's vineyard will find themselves out in the cold. *The Parable of the Wedding Feast* (*Matthew 22:1-14*) also showed how the most "deserving" lost out entirely. *The Parable of the Ten Girls* (*Matthew 25:1-13*) seems to praise an unwillingness to share. Likewise, *The Shrewd Manager* (*Luke 16:1-8*) seems to praise cunning. These are not the type of parables that the early church would invent if they wanted to win converts.

His other sayings and teachings were, for the most part, impossible to follow and utterly humbling for anyone who would try to follow them. He taught, "Sell all you have," "Give alms of all that you have," "Turn the other cheek," and "Give to anyone who asks." It seemed as if Jesus didn't want any followers. Who would anyone want to be part of a religion that required *everything*? No one who wanted to promote their new religion would create such teachings, least of all the Early Church, which understandably would want to make its teachings appealing, especially to their surrounding culture, which often threatened persecution. Evidently, these difficult teachings had been recorded as such, because these were exactly what Jesus had taught.

THE CRYPTIC NATURE OF JESUS' TEACHINGS

Jesus had been very cryptic about many of the central doctrines of the faith – His Messiah-ship, His Divinity, the Atonement, and the New Covenant. Had the early church edited the Gospels, they would have placed these cherished foundational doctrines more explicitly in the mouth of Jesus. His words would have reflected their concerns. However, for the most part, He had been embarrassingly silent about these doctrines until the time of His departure.

For example, Jesus only covertly confessed that He is the Messiah and that He is God. However, during His trial, in order to enable the Sanhedrin to convict Him, He confessed His messiah-ship by citing two messianic texts in reference to Himself (*Matthew 26:64*).

Capitalizing on Jesus' relative silence, liberal skeptics claim that the Gospels were written by the early church (70-100 AD) in order to prove that Jesus is actually God. Most critics will cite the Gospel of John, considered the latest Gospel. It makes more *explicit* references to Jesus' deity than the other three Gospels. Consequently, it reflects the church's growing desire to prove that Jesus is God.

For an extreme example, New Testament critic Bart Ehrman claims:

- The idea that Jesus was divine was a later Christian invention, one found, among our Gospels, only in John. (Ehrman, 249)

Ehrman believes that the last Gospel, John's, would have the most to say about the deity of Christ, because, at this point, the Church had fully evolved into this belief. Meanwhile, Ehrman claims that the earliest Gospel, Mark's Gospel, according to him, had nothing to say about Christ's deity, because the church had not yet evolved to the point of worshiping Jesus as God. In this regard, Ehrman makes an extravagantly erroneous claim:

- There is not one word in this Gospel about Jesus actually being God. (Ehrman, 247)

However, this assertion is contradicted by a multitude Markan verses. Even in the first three verses of his Gospel, Mark applies *Isaiah 40:3* ("Yahweh" coming to Israel) to Jesus' coming, equating Jesus with "Yahweh!"

Nevertheless, Jesus' *relative* silence about His deity, messianic mission, inaugurating the New Covenant, and even substitutionary atonement is embarrassing because it leaves many with the impression that Jesus, at least superficially, had preached a different Gospel than Peter, Paul and John. The teachings of Jesus, therefore, couldn't have been an invention of the Early Church, which would have wanted to seamlessly harmonize all of these teachings.

APPARENT CONTRADICTIONS

Had the early church exercised editorial oversight over the Gospels, they would have surely smoothed over the *apparent* contradictions between Jesus' teachings and the Epistles. However, we have no evidence that this ever happened, certainly not in any systematic way. Here are a couple of examples. Jesus seemed to teach unrestrained giving:

- Give to the one who asks you, and do not turn away from the one who wants to borrow from you. (*Matthew 5:42*)

However, the Epistles have more qualifications:

- For even when we were with you, we gave you this rule: "If a man will not work, he shall not eat. (*2 Thessalonians 3:10*)

Of course, Paul does not refer to the man who cannot work, but the one who *will not*. Nevertheless, to the casual reader, this seems like a contradiction, since Jesus didn't provide any exceptions. Had the early church written the Gospels to suit themselves, it is likely that they would have doctored Jesus' teachings to line up with the Epistles, but they didn't.

Jesus even seems to contradict Himself. On the one hand, it seemed as if He taught complete non-resistance to evil:

- But I tell you, 'Do not resist an evil person. If someone strikes you on the right cheek, turn to him the other also.' (*Matthew 5:39*)

However, He also proved to be very confrontational. He drove the money-changers out of the temple (*John 2:12-16; Matthew 21:12-13; Mark 11:15-17; Luke 19:45-46*) and confronted the religious leadership with charges of hypocrisy on many occasions. He also seemed to affirm the strenuous defense of one's family (*Matthew 24:43*).

Of course, these accounts can be reconciled, but to the casual reader, they seem like contradictions. If the early church had they edited the Gospels, it seems unlikely that they would have allowed these *apparent* contradictions to stand.

TROUBLING PROPHECIES

In many instances, it seems as if Jesus' prophecies had not been fulfilled. Adam Gopnik wrote:

- The Jesus faith begins with a failure of faith. His father let him down, and the promise wasn't kept: 'Some who are standing here will not taste death before they see the kingdom of God' [Matthew 16:28; Mark 9:1; Luke 9:27], Jesus announced, but none of them did. (www.newyorker.com)

However, each one of these promises is followed by an account of the Transfiguration on Mt. Tabor, where three of

Jesus' disciples viewed the glorified Christ – in a sense, the Kingdom of God.

However, other prophecies present us with more difficulty. On several occasions, Jesus seemed to prophesy His speedy return. When He sent His disciples out on their first evangelistic outreach, He promised them:

- When you are persecuted in one place, flee to another. I tell you the truth, you will not finish going through the cities of Israel before the Son of Man comes. (*Matthew 10:23*)

Regarding this perplexing prophecy, Albert Schweitzer claimed that Jesus had wrongly believed that He would return and set up His everlasting kingdom prior to the return of His disciples:

- He tells them in plain words…that He does not expect to see them back in the present age. However, was this really what Jesus had communicated? It seems highly unlikely. The preceding verses reveal that His return would be *preceded* by many global events:

- Be on your guard against men; they will hand you over to the local councils and flog you in their synagogues. On my account you will be brought before governors and kings as witnesses to them and to the Gentiles…Brother will betray brother to death, and a father his child; children will rebel against their parents and have them put to death. ALL men will hate you because of me, but he who stands firm to the end will be saved. (*Matthew 10:17-22*)

Instead, it seems that Jesus was preparing His disciples for both a long wait and possibly martyrdom. What then did Jesus intend to convey when He stated that "you will not finish going through the cities of Israel before the Son of Man comes?" (*Matthew 10:23*)

I think that Jesus, so thoroughly imbued with the prophecies of the Hebrew Scriptures, mimicked them. Often, these prophecies would begin with the immediate in view but would then jump years into the future in the same breath. Here's a familiar example – the prophecy to Abraham:

- "Leave your country, your people and your father's household and go to the land I will show you. I will make you into a great nation and I will bless you; I will make your name great, and you will be a blessing. I will bless those who bless you, and whoever curses you I will curse; and all peoples on earth will be blessed through you." (*Genesis 12:1-3*)

Although this prophecy had some immediate applications, the blessing to "all the peoples of the earth" would come *much later*.

Similarly, it seems that Jesus' prophecy to His disciple would also be realized by *later* generations.

He delivered a similar prophecy to the high priest:

- But Jesus remained silent. The high priest said to him, "I charge you under oath by the living God: Tell us if you are the Christ, the Son of God." "Yes, it is as you say," Jesus replied. "But I say to all of you: In the future you will see the Son of Man sitting at the right hand of the Mighty One and coming on the clouds of heaven." (*Matthew 26:63-64*)

This shouldn't be interpreted to mean that the high priest *himself* would see this take place. However, in harmony with the character of Hebrew prophecy, He was probably suggesting that the *Jewish people* would observe His return.

Perhaps the most fought-over prophecy about Jesus' return comes from *Matthew 24:34*, after Jesus had described the signs preceding His return:

- I tell you the truth, this generation will certainly not pass away until all these things have happened. (*Matthew 24:34*; also *Mark 13:30-31* and *Luke 21:32-33*)

"This generation" seems to take away any ambiguity about His return. Specifically, it would be during "this generation!" However, there is some controversy about what "this generation" really refers to. As we found in *Matthew 10*, here too we find that Jesus clearly doesn't believe that the end is near:

- You will hear of wars and rumors of wars, but see to it that you are not alarmed. Such things must happen, but the end is STILL TO COME. Nation will rise against nation, and kingdom against kingdom. There will be famines and earthquakes in various places. All these are the BEGINNING of birth pains. Then you will be handed over to be persecuted and put to DEATH [Evidently, the Apostles will not be living at the time of His return!], and you will be hated by all nations because of me. At that time many will turn away from the faith and will betray and hate each other, and MANY false prophets will appear and deceive many people. Because of the increase of wickedness, the love of most will grow cold…And this gospel of the kingdom will be preached in the WHOLE world as a testimony to all nations, and then the end will come. (*Matthew 24:6-14*)

101

Many things must first take place – martyrdom, apostasy, and worldwide evangelism - prior to Jesus' return. Therefore, "this generation" shouldn't be interpreted in its usual sense.

It is therefore more likely that "this generation" should be understood as "this Jewish people." In other words, Jesus seems to be saying that the Jewish people will still exist when He returns.

However, while the Greek word for "generation" ("genea") can be understood in certain verses in this sense (*Luke 11:50-51; Matthew 12:39*), only in the Hebrew Scriptures can we find the corresponding term ("dor"), usually rendered at "generation," used *unequivocally* in this manner:

- There they are, overwhelmed with dread, for God is present in the company ["dor"] of the righteous. *(Psalm 14:5)*

- By oppression and judgment he was taken away. And who can speak of his descendants ["dor"]? For he was cut off from the land of the living; for the transgression of my people he was stricken. (*Isaiah 53:8*)

In both of these cases, "dor" cannot be understood as "generation" – a typical human lifespan. In Isaiah, "dor" can only be understood as the *many* generations, "descendants," or people who didn't come forth from the Messiah, because He died for the sins of the people.

Was Jesus mistaken about the time of His return? Well, if we choose to understand His words as indicating an early return, then it does seem that He was mistaken. However, if we don't dismiss the entire context of His remarks, then it is not possible to construe His words as prophesying an early return.

Nevertheless, these prophecies are troubling and have understandably invited the charge that Jesus had been mistaken. Why then would the Gospels have retained such troubling prophecies? The writers must have regarded them as genuine!

New Testament scholar, Craig Blomberg, consequently concluded,

- Whether by giving the Gospels the benefit of the doubt which all narratives of purportedly historical events merit or by approaching them with initial suspicion in which every detail must satisfy the criteria of authenticity, the verdict should remain the same. The Gospels may be accepted as trustworthy accounts of what Jesus did and said. (*The Historical Reliability of the Gospels*)

If the Gospels are reliable, then we can accept their accounts of the miraculous, especially the Resurrection. If Jesus rose from the dead, this authenticates His testimony about Himself and His words as the Words of God Himself. It also authenticates His promise about the inviolability of His own words:

- Heaven and earth will pass away, but my words will not pass away. (*Matthew 24:35*)

Hallelujah!

WORKS CITED

Bishop, James, (3/20/17), *"58 Scholar Quotes on Jesus' Miracles"*
www.reasonsforjesus.com/58-scholar-quote-jesus-miracles/

Blomberg, Craig L., *The Historical Reliability of the Gospels,* (IVP Press, 2011)

Ehrman, Bart, *Jesus Interrupted*, (NYC: Harper Collins, 2009)

Gopnik, Adam, (5/24/19) *"What Did Jesus Do?"*
www.newyorker.com/magazine/2010/05/24/what-did-jesus-do

Chapter 10

THE HEBREW SCRIPTURES: AFFIRMED BY CHRIST

We have no warrant to believe that Scripture is the Word of God ("God-breathed" as Paul wrote in *2 Timothy 3:16-17*) unless Scripture instructs us to believe this. This raises the question, "What did Jesus teach regarding the Scriptures?" Jesus consistently treated Scripture, both directly and indirectly (through His quotations of Scripture) as God's very words.

For one thing, Jesus totally subordinated Himself under God's Word. He never said, "These are my teachings, not God's." When tempted by the Devil, He relied exclusively on Scripture:

- Jesus answered, It is written: 'Man does not live on bread alone, but on every word that comes from the mouth of God.' (*Matthew 4:4*)

If Jesus relied on Scripture when tempted, so must we! He also ruled against any picking-and-choosing among the verses, by stating that we are to live by "EVERY word that comes from the mouth of God." It seems that Jesus regarded every word of Scripture as coming from God.

Jesus did not set Himself above Scripture as its judge to decide which verses were truly inspired. He received it all as God's Word:

- Do not think that I have come to abolish the Law or the Prophets; I have not come to abolish them but to fulfill them. I tell you the truth, until heaven and earth disappear, not the smallest letter, not the least stroke of a pen, will by any means disappear from the Law until everything is accomplished. (*Matthew 5:17-18*)

If Jesus had regarded the Word as errant in some respect, He would never have said "until EVERYTHING is accomplished." Instead, He might have said, "Until every part that is *without error* is accomplished." Rather, He continually insisted that *everything* had to be fulfilled. To those He had encountered on the road to Emmaus:

- He said..."How foolish you are, and how slow of heart to believe ALL that the prophets have spoken! Did not the Christ have to suffer these things and then enter his glory?" And beginning with Moses and all the Prophets, he explained to them what was said in all the Scriptures concerning himself... He said to them, "This is what I told you while I was still with you: EVERYTHING must be fulfilled that is written about me in the Law of Moses, the Prophets and the Psalms." Then he opened their minds so they could understand the Scriptures. (*Luke 24: 25-27, 44-45*)

Notice how Jesus opened their minds to understand the *Scriptures*, rather than His own Words. Whenever He quoted from the Scriptures, it was always affirming what Scripture had said. Never once did He disparage Scripture. Instead, He castigated those who didn't know the Scriptures:

- Jesus replied, "You are in error because you do not know the Scriptures or the power of God. (*Matthew 22:29*)

They didn't know Scripture because they didn't esteem it, despite their protestations to the contrary:

- But do not think I will accuse you [Pharisees] before the Father. Your accuser is Moses, on whom your hopes

106

are set. If you believed Moses, you would believe me, for he wrote about me. But since you do not believe what he wrote, how are you going to believe what I say? (*John 5:45-47*)

In contrast to the religious leadership, Jesus believed in what Moses had written and that Scripture could not be broken" (*John 10:35*). He even regarded the Psalms as ultimately authored by God. Quoting from *Psalm 110*, Jesus claimed that David was "speaking by the Spirit":

- He said to them, "How is it then that David, speaking by the Spirit, calls him 'Lord'? (*Matthew 22:43*)

Never once did Jesus raise the question about the divine origin (OF) a single verse. Consequently, if we want to call ourselves a "Christian," we cannot disparage Jesus' teachings about Scripture.

This is something many do by claiming that the first chapters of Genesis are not historical. However, Jesus quoted from the first two chapters as historical:

- He [Jesus] answered [the Pharisees regarding divorce], "Have you not read that he who created them from the beginning made them male and female [quoting *Genesis 1:26-27*], and said, 'Therefore a man shall leave his father and his mother and hold fast to his wife, and the two shall become one flesh' [*Genesis 2:24*]! So they are no longer two but one flesh. What therefore God has [historically] joined together, let not man separate." (*Matthew 19:4-6*)

Had not God historically and realistically joined together the man and the woman, Jesus' argument against divorce would have fallen apart.

107

If we are to live faithfully with our Savior, we must submit to His teaching as He did to those of His Father. If we refuse to accept His teachings about Scripture, we also refuse to be His children.

How did Jesus regard His own teachings? Did He regard them as Scripture? Even though He consistently submitted to what had been written, Jesus also regarded His Words as Scripture. During His Olivet Discourse, He proclaimed:

- Heaven and earth will pass away, but my words will not pass away. (*Matthew 24:35*)

His Words were as unassailable as were the Words of the Scriptures (*Matthew 5:16-18*). Consequently, in the midst of His Great Commission, He instructed His Apostles:

- Go therefore and make disciples of all nations, baptizing them in the name of the Father and of the Son and of the Holy Spirit, teaching them to observe all that I have commanded you. (*Matthew 28:19-20; John 14:26*)

Instead of commanding them to teach the Torah, he commanded His Apostles to teach "all that I have commanded you." No Prophet of Israel had commanded this. Such a command could only come from God.

How did His Apostles and those who had written under Apostolic guidance regard these same Scriptures? Did they regard them in the same way that their Master had? Yes! Whenever they quoted or alluded to the Hebrew Scriptures, never did they disparage or question them. Instead, their citations always fell in line with the maxim, that "if the Scriptures said it, that settles it."

This should also settle the question for us. However, it doesn't seem that Jesus was able to affirm the words of the NT books, but the next chapter will attempt to address this issue.

Chapter 11

THE NEW TESTAMENT: AFFIRMED BY CHRIST

It seems that the New Testament books became Scripture as soon as they were written and received by the various churches! How do we know this? Well, for one thing, Jesus had commissioned His Apostles to do this very thing:

- But when the Helper comes, whom I will send to you from the Father, the Spirit of truth, who proceeds from the Father, he will bear witness about me. And you also will bear witness, because you have been with me from the beginning. (John 15:26-27)

The Apostles were commissioned to teach the Gospel in two ways. They would testify of what they had seen and experienced, and the Spirit would also provide the rest. But how?

- But the Helper, the Holy Spirit, whom the Father will send in my name, he will teach you ALL things and bring to your remembrance ALL that I have said to you. (*John 14:26*)

According to Jesus, the Apostolic message would be the product of the Spirit. The Spirit would make up for their (the Apostles) inability to understand Christ's teachings and would make the New Testament writings His own (*2 Peter 1:19-21*):

- I still have many things to say to you, but you cannot bear them now. When the Spirit of truth comes, he will guide you into ALL the truth, for he will not speak on his own authority, but whatever he hears he will speak, and he will declare to you the things that are to come. He will glorify me, for he will take what is mine and declare it to you. (*John 16:12-14*)

The Spirit would supernaturally impart all knowledge to them. Jesus subsequently sent them off into the world with His Gospel:

- Go therefore and make disciples of all nations, baptizing them in the name of the Father and of the Son and of the Holy Spirit, teaching them to observe ALL that I have commanded you. And behold, I am with you always, to the end of the age. (*Matthew 28:19-20*)

He expected a lot of them. They had to teach ALL that they had been taught. However, Jesus never explicitly specified whether their teaching was to be only verbal or whether it was to also include the written Word. However, Jesus did claim that His Words would never pass away (*Matthew 24:35*), indicating that He environed the New Testament. In either case, their calling could only be accomplished by Divine assistance, and the Apostles also understood this:

- Now we have received not the spirit of the world, but the Spirit who is from God, that we might understand the things freely given us by God. And we impart this in words not taught by human wisdom but TAUGHT BY THE SPIRIT, interpreting spiritual truths to those who are spiritual. (*1 Corinthians 2:12-13*)

According to Paul, since the entirety of the Gospel came from above, it was entirely God-breathed:

- All Scripture is breathed out by God and profitable for teaching, for reproof, for correction, and for training in righteousness, that the man of God may be complete, equipped for every good work. (*2 Timothy 3:16-17*)

Because it was entirely God-breathed, it was able to make "the man of God...complete, equipped for every good work." Had there been any human inaccuracies in the originals, this could not have been asserted.

How did the early Church know that the Apostolic teachings were all God-breathed? The fact that the Apostles had been divinely commissioned by our Lord to bring the Gospel to the world had been made plain to all through God's miraculous attestations, which put His stamp-of-approval on His Apostles:

- How shall we escape if we neglect such a great salvation? It was declared at first by the Lord, and it was attested to us by those who heard, while God also bore witness by signs and wonders and various miracles and by gifts of the Holy Spirit distributed according to his will. (*Hebrews 2:3-4*)

These signs and wonders accompanied the Apostles in order to validate their divine commission before the Church, and the Church got the message:

- And they devoted themselves to the apostles' teaching and the fellowship, to the breaking of bread and the prayers. And awe came upon every soul, and many wonders and signs were being done through the APOSTLES. (*Acts 2:42-43*)

It therefore was clear to all that the Apostles were teaching with the authority of God Himself in accordance with the commission of their Savior Jesus. It was also these signs that had enabled Paul to declare that he too was speaking and writing the very words of God:

- The signs of a true apostle were performed among you with utmost patience, with signs and wonders and mighty works. (*2 Corinthians 12:12*)

These miracles were unmistakably divine validations – signs that God approved of Paul's teaching:

- So they remained for a long time, speaking boldly for the Lord, who bore witness to the word of his grace, granting signs and wonders to be done by their hands. (*Acts 14:3*)

- And God was doing extraordinary miracles by the hands of Paul, so that even handkerchiefs or aprons that had touched his skin were carried away to the sick, and their diseases left them and the evil spirits came out of them. (*Acts 19:11-12*)

Consequently, there was never any doubt in the early Church that Paul's 13 letters were each the Word of God. And they were received accordingly.

Some scholars claim that the Apostles would never have believed that they were writing Scripture. However, this claim does not accord with the Scriptural evidence. Clearly, Paul knew that he was penning the Word of God:

- Yet among the mature we do impart wisdom, although it is not a wisdom of this age or of the rulers of this age, who are doomed to pass away. But we impart a secret and hidden wisdom of God, which God decreed before the ages for our glory. (*1 Corinthians 2:6-7*)

- If anyone thinks that he is a prophet, or spiritual, he should acknowledge that the things I am writing to you are a COMMAND OF THE LORD. (*1 Corinthians 14:37*)

Not only did Paul declare his writings to be Scripture, he also claimed that this Word could supernaturally transform:

- And we also thank God constantly for this, that when you received the word of God, which you heard from us, you accepted it not as the word of men but as what it really is, the word of God, which is at work in you believers. (*1 Thessalonians 2:13*)

Consequently, his letters were received as Scripture and were copied and carried around to other churches (*1 Thessalonians 5:27; Colossians 4:16*). Evidently, the various churches regarded his writings as Scripture as soon as they were received.

Peter also regarded his writings as the commandments of the Lord:

- You should remember the predictions of the holy prophets and the commandment of the Lord and Savior THROUGH YOUR APOSTLES, (*2 Peter 3:2*)

Peter also regarded Paul's writings as Scripture (*2 Peter 3:15-16*). And John regarded his as Scripture:

- I warn everyone who hears the words of the prophecy of this book: if anyone adds to them, God will add to him the plagues described in this book, and if anyone takes away from the words of the book of this prophecy, God will take away his share in the tree of life and in the holy city, which are described in this book. (*Revelation 22:18-19*)

John could only issue such a warning if he was convinced that what he had written was Scripture.

The Apostles evidently understood that Jesus' commission for them to teach the Gospel also pertained to their writings, as much as it also did to the Hebrew Scriptures, which all regarded as the product of the Spirit. The Churches didn't have to wait for a Church Council for them to adopt the Apostolic writings as Scripture. No expert pronunciation was necessary. Instead, the Lord had made their writings, authored of the Spirit, plain to the Church.

Clearly, only the Apostles had such authority among the first century churches. Consequently, there was only one way to exert influence among the churches - to pose as an Apostle, attaching an Apostle's name to their *own* pseudonymous (falsely named) letters. And this is exactly what many imposters did.

Therefore, Paul warned the Church against such early forgeries (2 *Thessalonians 2:2; 3:17; 1 Corinthians16:21; Galatians 6:11; Colossians 4:18*). Such a warning would only be appropriate if his own letters carried significant, even divine, authority among the churches.

Consequently, it wasn't until about 200 after the Cross that the Church began to seek further assurances for seven of the Epistles. The other 20 books of the New Testament were never questioned. The witness of the early Church in their recognition of the Spirit-given Apostolic writings was that unified!

While it is true that the *formal* identification of the 27 books of the New Testament was not complete until the late 4th century, by every other indication, the early churches, had, from the beginning, received these 27 as Scripture. We have no record that any Church Father disputed any of the 27 books until the third century.

Why the later debate regarding the other seven books? Norman L. Geisler and William E. Nix explain:

- The noted biblical scholar B. F. Westcott observed, "Its general agreement with our own [canon] is striking and important; and its omissions admit of easy explanation." The omitted books were originally destined for the Western [Latin] world, and the Syrian church was in the East. The distance and lack of verifying communications slowed down the final acceptance of these books in the Eastern Bible [*The Old Syriac Translation*], which had come out before that evidence was available to them. (Geisler/Nix, *109-110*)

The opposite was also true. The Western world had not received all of the books that the Eastern world had initially received. Communications between the two worlds had no doubt been interrupted by intense persecutions. Nevertheless, according to Geisler and Nix, the two worlds combined had received all of the 27 New Testament books:

- Between the two earliest Bibles in the Christian Church there is recognition of the canonicity of all twenty-seven New Testament books. (Geisler/Nix, 110)

What was this early recognition based upon? The Early Church had been convinced by the miraculous confirmatory attestations that if a book was Apostolic, it was Scripture. Therefore, the canon was not a matter of political/ecclesiastical maneuvering but of the sovereign work of God.

Had Jesus commissioned the Apostles to write Scripture?
We have already seen that He had commissioned His Apostles to go throughout the world carrying His teachings. However, did He also have His written teachings in mind? He must have! How do we know this? For one thing, in His Olivet

Discourse about the end and His evidential return, He claimed that His Words would never disappear:

- Heaven and earth will pass away, but my words will not pass away. (*Matthew 24:35*)

His Apostles would disappear but not Jesus' Words. How could this be unless He had envisioned or instructed them to be written! Evidently, the Apostles had been convinced that He had also ordained their written as well as their verbal ministry.

If Jesus had prepared the way for the canon of the New Testament, we should find some tangible evidence for this, and we do. We find that the early churches were copying the individual books for dissemination:

- All twenty-seven books of the New Testament were written, copied, and began to be distributed among the churches before the close of the first century. In the first half of the second century…almost every book of the New Testament was explicitly cited as Scripture. (Geisler/Nix, 155)

Evidently, the canonization process started immediately. One indication of this is the authoritative citations from these 27 books by the Church Fathers:

- By the end of the first century some fourteen books of the New Testament were cited. By A.D. 110 there were nineteen books recognized by citation. And within another forty years (A.D. 150) some twenty-four New Testament books were acknowledged. Before the century ended, which is about one hundred years after the New Testament was written, twenty-six books were cited. (Geisler/Nix, 157)

- Not only did the early Fathers cite all twenty-seven books of the New Testament, they also quoted virtually all of the verses in all of these twenty-seven books. (Geisler/Nix, 157)

Lists and manuscripts containing the accepted books of the New Testament also began to appear.

But how do we know that we have the right Gospels – Matthew, Mark, Luke and John? Skepticism about this was given new life in 1946 when the Gnostic Gospels (GG) were uncovered at an Egyptian site – Nag Hammadi. Although we had already known about these "gospels" from the writings of the Church Fathers, who excoriated them, this was the first time that scholars actually had many of them in hand.

Since then, some extreme voices have declared that these "gospels" are just as valid as the Biblical ones. Dan Brown's fictional work, *The Da Vinci Code*, even theorized that the church had used all of these "gospels" until the Council of Nicea (315 AD) when they were finally banned. However, there are many compelling reasons for confidence in the four Canonical Gospels (CG):

1. **The GG's reflect a theology alien to the Bible and more in line with Greek and Eastern thought.** For instance, they maintain that the creation is evil, created by an evil sub-god. This directly contradicts the Biblical creation account which holds that God had regarded the creation as "very good" (*Genesis 1:31*). In contrast, the CG's do not contradict the Hebrew Scriptures – exactly what we'd expect to find if God is the author of all.

2. **The GG's are all pseudonymous – deceptively attributed to an Apostle.** This was clearly a device used in hope of gaining acceptance within the church.

In contrast, the CG's are all unnamed. Seemingly, they had nothing to prove and were concerned more about truth than in gaining acceptance or personal notoriety.

3. **The GG's are consistently dated late into the 2nd century and after, and therefore could never have been regarded as Apostolic or as eyewitness accounts.** In contrast, the CG's are all dated within the 1st century, even by the skeptics. One liberal scholar, J.A.T. Robinson had dated the CG's 40-65 AD. The Church Fathers all contend that the Gospels were Apostolic. Consistent with this, they claim that Mark's Gospel recorded Peter's eyewitness accounts, while Luke's Gospel reflects Paul's sermons.

4. **The CG's were universally accepted by the church.** There was never any indication that the church had ever questioned any of the four. In contrast, the GG's were accepted by *none*! There is no ancient Bible manuscript that contains any of them alongside with other NT writings. The only times that a Church Father quoted them was to criticize them. Even the Gnostic philosophers never cited them as canonical. Nor did they write commentaries on them. Meanwhile, they did write commentaries on a couple of the CG's!

5. **The Gnostic philosophers cite the NT CG's as authoritative.** One Gnostic philosopher, Marcion 160 AD, identified his "bible" as containing simply the Gospel of Luke and ten of Paul's Epistles. None of the Gnostics ever cited GG's as part of their bible.

6. **While all of the ancient canonical lists contain the four CG's, they never contain any of the GG.**

7. **The Gnostics either claimed that they had been privileged to have received secret knowledge from**

the Apostles or from within. However, they were never able to produce any evidence of such a transmission of material. Nor is there any evidence that the GGs were ever part of anyone's church. In fact, the Church Father Irenaeus (180 AD) attempted to check out their claims by interviewing a number of church elders who would have knowledge of any secret transmission of teachings. However, he reports that they were all unaware of any such teachings.

8. **The CG's are all God-centered.** As such, even the Apostles are portrayed in a disparaging light. Clearly, the CG's are not self-promoting, but instead, seem committed to presenting a factual picture of the life of Jesus. In contrast, the GGs are very self-promoting – a quality that makes them less trustworthy. It is only the spiritually enlightened who are capable of understanding their secret message and of being saved.

9. **The GGs disappeared, while the CG's remained.** The Bible declares that the Word of God endures forever (*Isaiah 40:8*). This certainly could not be said about the GGs!

Our Lord has promised that He would protect His Word (*Matthew 24:35; Isaiah 40:8*), and He has. Although humans played a significant role in the writing and preserving of the books of the New Testament Canon, by all indications, our Lord exercised sovereign oversight over the entire process.

WORKS CITED

Geisler, Norman L and Nix, William E, *From God to Us: How we Got our Bible*, (Chicago: Moody Press, 2012)

Chapter 12

THE RESURRECTION

Jesus had the highest possible regard for Scripture. According to Him, it was entirely the Word of God. Not the slightest marking of Scripture had been misplaced. (*Matthew 5:17-18*)

However, why should we accept His testimony? Perhaps He was in error or even deluded? However, if He is God-incarnate, then we can trust His testimony. But was He? Should we just take His word for it?

Jesus had instructed us to *not* believe in His words unless there was also evidence to confirm them:

- If I am not doing the works [miracles] of my Father, then do not believe me; but if I do them, even though you do not believe me, believe the works, that you may know and understand that the Father is in me and I am in the Father. (*John 10:37-38*; also *John 5:31-38*)

His entire ministry was bathed in the most incredible miracles. But the miracle that confirmed His words and the Words of the Hebrew Scriptures more than any other miracle was the Resurrection. If Jesus rose from the dead, as He said that He would, this unique event confirms His other words, namely, His teachings about the divinity of the Scriptures.

The proof that He had risen from the dead is quite impressive. In the *"Resurrection of the Son of God"*, N.T. Wright, the Bishop of Durham, England wrote:

- The proposal that Jesus was bodily raised from the dead possesses unrivalled power to explain the historical data at the heart of early Christianity. (Strobel, 104)

121

It is the evidence that gives this claim "unrivalled power." Here is how I hope to lay out the evidence:

1. **Jesus was crucified.**
2. **His tomb was empty and no one was able to produce His body.**
3. **Many eyewitnesses testified that He had risen.**
4. **The circumstantial evidence also confirms His Resurrection.**
5. **No other theory has been able to account for these facts.**

1.   Jesus was crucified.

Even Bible skeptics have called this an "indisputable fact":

- NT scholar, John Dominic Crossan: "That He was crucified is as sure as anything historical ever can be." (Strobel, 113)

- Both Gerd Ludemann, an atheistic NT critic, and Bart Ehrman, who's an agnostic, call the crucifixion an indisputable fact. (Strobel, 113)

- Tacitus, Roman historian (110 AD): "Jesus suffered the extreme penalty under the reign of Tiberius." (Strobel, 113)

- Josephus [the Jewish historian, 90 AD] reports that Pilate 'condemned him to be crucified'…Even the Jewish Talmud reports that 'Yeshu was hanged.' (Strobel, 113)

- Apologist Michael Licona claims that "Lucian of Samosata, who was a Greek satirist, mentions the crucifixion, and Mara Bar-Serapion, who was a pagan, confirms Jesus was executed." (Strobel, 113)

Even the skeptics endorse the fact that Jesus died on the cross:

- The crucifixion of Jesus is recognized even by the skeptical Jesus Seminar as "one indisputable fact." (www.leaderu.com)

Michael Licona claims that "The scholarly consensus—again, even among those who are skeptical about the Resurrection— is absolutely overwhelming." Nevertheless, six hundred years after the event, the Qur'an claimed that a look-alike died in Jesus' place, "and Allah raised him [Jesus] up to Himself." However, this assertion does not rest upon any historical evidence. (Strobel, 133)

2.   Jesus' tomb was empty, and no one was able to produce His body.

Had Jesus' body been produced, any claim of a resurrection would have easily been dismissed.

All early reports, even Jewish ones cited an "empty tomb"! However, there are no reports of anyone producing His body, although the Jews and Romans had every reason to produce it. Had it been produced, Christians wouldn't have been able to believe in a resurrected Christ. Besides this, had His body been produced, the thousands who came to faith after Pentecost would instead have mocked such a faith.

To guard against the possibility that Jesus' disciples might say that He rose from the dead, the Jewish leadership prevailed upon Pilate to provide a Roman guard at Jesus' tomb. However, even with the guard, the chief priests claimed that the disciples stole the body:

- Now while they were going, behold, some of the guard came into the city and reported to the chief priests all the things that had happened. When they had assembled with the elders and consulted together, they gave a large sum of money to the soldiers, saying, "Tell them, 'His disciples came at night and stole Him away while we slept.' And if this comes to the governor's ears, we will appease him and make you secure." So they took the money and did as they were instructed; and this saying is commonly reported among the Jews until this day. (*Matthew 28:11-15*)

Even Justin Martyr (150 AD) wrote in his "*Dialogue with Trypho*" that the Jews still sent ambassadors throughout the Mediterranean, claiming that the "Disciples stole the body." However, for a number of reasons, this doesn't seem to be possible:

- The disciples had been running scared prior to the Resurrection. They wouldn't have risked their lives for a dangerous prank. Besides, they would never have died as martyrs for a story that they had cooked up.

- They had no motive to deceive and to risk martyrdom themselves.

- They could not have stolen away the body under the watchful eyes of the Roman guard.

- Had the Jewish authorities produced the body, they would have easily put the kibosh on this fledgling faith.

There is no indication in the Gospels themselves that this was all part of a subterfuge. Instead, their accounts that women were the first to see the risen Christ also argue against this. Why? The testimony of women had been disregarded in Jewish culture at this time. For example, the Jewish historian Josephus (90 AD) wrote:

- But let not the testimony of women be admitted, on account of the levity and boldness of their sex."(Strobel, 124)

Willian Lane Craig reasons that the empty tomb could not have been a legend:

- If the empty tomb story were a legend, then it is most likely that the male disciples would have been made the first to discover the empty tomb. The fact that despised women, whose testimony was deemed worthless, were the chief witnesses to the fact of the empty tomb can only be plausibly explained if, like it or not, they actually were the discoverers of the empty tomb. (www.desiringgod.org)

According to Strobel, "Gary Habermas determined that about 75% [of historians] on the subject [of the empty tomb] regard it as an historical fact." He adds, "All the strictly historical evidence we have is in favor [of the empty tomb], and those scholars who reject it ought to recognize that they do so on some other ground than that of scientific history." (Strobel, 123)

D.H. Van Daalen confirmed this assessment:

- It is extremely difficult to object to the empty tomb on historical grounds; those who deny it do so on the basis of theological or philosophical assumptions. (Van Daalen, 41)

NT critic Jacob Kremer, who has specialized in the study of the resurrection, claimed:

- "By far most exegetes hold firmly to the reliability of the biblical statements about the empty tomb" and he lists twenty-eight scholars to back up his fantastic claim. (www.desiringgod.org)

The Early Church worshipped on the Sunday – the Resurrection Day – rather than on the Jewish Sabbath (Saturday). Evidently, they were convinced that Jesus' tomb was empty and that He rose on Sunday. How else to explain the change from the Sabbath day!

3.   Many eyewitnesses testified that He had risen.

The Disciples believed that Jesus had appeared to them. Their assertions about this event are quite numerous and credible:

- This is the uniform testimony of all 27 books of the New Testament! Licona states that, "Even very liberal scholars will concede that we have four biographies [Gospels] written within 70 years of Jesus' life that unambiguously report the disciples' claims that Jesus rose from the dead." (Strobel, 83)

- Preserved oral tradition is also in agreement. According to Licona, the NT "preserves several sermons of the apostles…We can say that the vast majority of historians believe that the early apostolic teachings are enshrined in these sermons summaries in Acts – and they declare that Jesus rose bodily from the dead.

This is also the uniform testimony of all the Church Fathers. For example, Clement (95 AD) wrote:

- Therefore, having received orders and complete certainty caused by the resurrection of our Lord Jesus Christ and believing in the Word of God, they went with the Holy Spirit's certainty. (1 Clement 42:3)

The Church Father Polycarp (110 AD) wrote:

- For they did not love the present age, but Him who died for our benefit and for our sake was raised by God. (*Polycarp's Letter to the Philippians 9:2*)

It's apparent that Christians have practiced baptism and communion from the very inception of the Church. These rituals testify to the fact that they acknowledged the death and Resurrection of Christ.

There are several things that make the apostolic testimonies of the Resurrection highly credible:

- Some of the Church Fathers, whose writings we still retain, knew the Apostles of Jesus. Many were also martyred for their insistence that Jesus rose.

- The Apostles "were willing to endure persecution and even martyrdom....The church fathers Clement, Polycarp, Ignatius, Tertullian, and Origen – they all confirm this. In fact, at least seven early sources testify that the disciples willingly suffered in defense of their beliefs – and if we include the martyrdoms of Paul and Jesus' half-brother James, we have eleven sources" (Licona, 85). They wouldn't have suffered for their testimony of the Resurrection unless they were convinced that it had actually happened.

- The Apostles presented themselves in a very unfavorable light in the NT writings. They must have been convinced of a greater and surpassing truth – the Resurrection – to be willing to make themselves look so ridiculous. If their testimony of the Resurrection had merely been fabrication, they would have had every reason to present a pristine portrait of themselves to the world.

- Their writings emerge with flying colors when examined culturally, critically and historically.

- Jesus appeared to His disciples over a 40-day period following His Resurrection. Paul reports that on one occasion, He appeared to over 500 at one time: "He appeared to Cephas, then to the twelve. After that He appeared to more than five hundred brethren at one time, most of whom remain until now, but some have fallen asleep; then He appeared to James, then to all the apostles; and last of all, as to one untimely born, He appeared to me also" (*1 Corinthians15:5-8*). Paul suggested, only about 20 years after the Resurrection that his readers could verify, through these eyewitnesses, whether these events really took place. Had they not taken place as Paul had reported, he would have been ridiculed and rejected.

- Jesus' Apostles weren't reporting about an event that had taken place in China, but in Jerusalem, where their testimonies could easily have been discredited. There certainly were enough people trying to do so.

- The Gospel accounts record that two members of the Sanhedrin had taken the body of Jesus and buried it. This could have easily been contradicted if it hadn't taken place. Likewise, many supernatural events accompanied the accounts of the Crucifixion – appearances by dead saints, darkness upon the land for three hours, the rending of the Temple veil, and an earthquake. Had these events not taken place, the Gospel accounts could easily have been falsified by the Jerusalem establishment, situated as they were in the very location of these events.

- The Gospels report that women were the first to testify of the Resurrection. However, no one would have fabricated such an account, because the testimony of women was disdained. Furthermore, Mary Magdalene seems to have been the first to report the Resurrection. However she had an additional onus upon her. She had been regarded as a sinner. The Apostles would never have fabricated such accounts.

- There is no record of the disciples ever recanting. If this had ever happened, such a record would surely have been preserved by the many adversaries of the Christian faith.

Licona reports that Gary Habermas had consulted over 2,000 scholarly sources on the Resurrection and concluded with Habermas that "probably no fact was more widely recognized than that the early Christian believers had real experiences that they thought were appearances of the risen Jesus." (Licona, 86). For instance:

- Even the atheist [Gerd] Lüdemann conceded: 'It may be taken as historically certain that Peter and the disciples had experiences after Jesus' death in which Jesus appeared to them as the risen Christ.'" (Lüdemann, 80).

The liberal Jewish historian, Paula Fredriksen, claims

- The Disciples' conviction that they had seen the risen Christ…is historical bedrock, facts known past doubting. (Strobel, 119)

- I know in their own terms what they saw was the raised Jesus. That's what they say and then all the historic evidence we have afterwards attests to their conviction that that's what they saw. I'm not saying that they really did see the raised Jesus. I wasn't there. I don't know what they saw. But I do know that as a historian that they must have seen something. (Strobel, 119)

However, as non-believers, they are more inclined to ascribe the disciples' sincere accounts of the Resurrection to hallucinations or visions. If so, they all experienced the very *same hallucination* during the 40 days of Jesus' appearances – 500 at one time – even hallucinations that included eating and talking with Jesus and even touching Him! Paul reported:

- For I delivered [this early report) to you as of first importance what I also received: that Christ died for our sins in accordance with the Scriptures, that he was buried, that he was raised on the third day in accordance with the Scriptures, and that he appeared to Cephas, then to the twelve. Then he appeared to more than five hundred brothers at one time, most of whom are still alive, though some have fallen asleep. Then he appeared to James, then to all the apostles. Last of all, as to one untimely born, he appeared also to me. (*1 Corinthians 15:3-8*)

Paul wrote (55-57 AD) that on one occasion, Jesus had appeared to "more than five hundred…most of whom are still alive." This leads to three conclusions:

1. It would have been hard to get away with such a statement had it not been true.

2. These people were still available to confirm Jesus' post-Resurrection appearances – something that would require confirmation.
3. Jesus must have risen. How else could the faith of unbelievers, like James and Paul, be explained, especially after the crucifixion!

NT scholar James Dunn is emphatic that Jesus' disciple had been convinced that Jesus had risen:

- It is an undoubted fact that the conviction that God had raised Jesus from the dead and had exalted Jesus to his right hand, transformed Jesus' first disciples and their beliefs about Jesus. (McDowell,14)

Christian Apologist Michael Licona adds:

- After Jesus' death, the disciples endured persecution, and a number of them experienced martyrdom. The strength of their conviction indicates that they were not just claiming Jesus had appeared to them after rising from the dead. They really believed it. They willingly endangered themselves by publicly proclaiming the risen Christ. (McDowell,16)

According to Christian Apologist Sean McDowell, the Resurrection had been the universal belief of the Church:

- From the Apostles forward, there is no evidence for an early Christian community that did not have belief in the Resurrection at its core. The centrality of the Resurrection can be seen by considering the earliest Christian creeds, the preaching in Acts, and the writings of the apostolic fathers. (McDowell,14)

4.   The circumstantial evidence also confirms His Resurrection.

EVIDENCE OF CONVERSIONS: The Apostle Paul had been the leading persecutor of the Church, leading lynching parties against them. However, he reports that he had had an encounter with Christ which blinded him. He was them miraculously healed and subsequently had other encounters with Christ. Had he not been convinced that Jesus had risen, there would have been no conversion. Licona concludes, "He had nothing to gain in the world – except his own suffering and martyrdom – for making this up."

Initially, Jesus' family had thought that "He is out of his mind" (Mark 3:21; John 7:3-5). This assessment would have been reinforced by the Crucifixion. However, James and Jude became believers. Had the Resurrection not taken place, it is hard to conceive how this transformation could have taken place.

Without the Resurrection, it is inconceivable that multitudes would have sacrificed everything for a disgraced "Messiah" who had been shamefully crucified. The *Book of Acts* reports that after Peter had preached his initial sermon, 3000 came to believe (*Acts 2:41*). Had there not been substantial evidence for the Resurrection, this could not have happened. No one would have risked persecution for a disgraced would-be Messiah.

The Gospels show us that, following the Crucifixion, the disciples had fled and abandoned their faith. Only the Resurrection could have convinced them that they had a future with Jesus and given them the boldness to stand against persecution.

Only the Resurrection could account for the growth of the Church. Had there been no Resurrection, only scorn and ridicule would accompany anyone who continued to believe in someone humiliated and crucified.

Dr. Simon Greenleaf, founder of the Harvard Law School, notes:

- "Propagating this new faith, even in the most inoffensive and peaceful manner, [early Christians received] contempt, opposition… and cruel deaths. Yet this faith they zealously did propagate, and all these miseries they endured undismayed, nay rejoicing. As one after another was put to a miserable death, the survivors only [continued] their work with increased vigor and resolution… The annals of military warfare afford scarcely an example of like heroic constancy, patience, and unflinching courage… If it were morally possible for them to have been deceived in this matter, every human motive operated to lead them to discover and avow their error. From these [considerations] there is no escape but in the perfect conviction and admission that they were good men, testifying to that which they had carefully observed…and well knew to be true. (www:christiananswers.net)

5.   No other theory has been able to account for these facts.

There have been many attempts to humanly explain the empty tomb. However, these have all failed. Philosopher and apologist William Lane Craig wrote:

- C. F. D. Moule of Cambridge University concludes that we have here a belief which nothing in terms of prior historical influences can account for--apart from the Resurrection itself.   (www.leaderu.com)

- Any responsible historian, then, who seeks to give an account of the matter, must deal with these four independently established facts: the honorable burial of Jesus, the discovery of his empty tomb, his appearances alive after his death, and the very origin of the disciples' belief in His Resurrection and, hence, of Christianity itself. I want to emphasize that these four facts represent, not the conclusions of conservative scholars, nor have I quoted conservative scholars, but represent rather the majority view of New Testament scholarship today. The question is: How do you best explain these facts?

Craig concludes that all of the naturalistic theories have now been rejected by modern scholarship. This leaves the Resurrection as the only contender:

- In fact, the evidence is so powerful that one of today's leading *Jewish* theologians Pinchas Lapide has declared himself convinced on the basis of the evidence that the God of Israel raised Jesus from the dead!

If Jesus rose from the dead, then this validates what He had said about Himself and about the Scriptures – that they could not be broken (*John 10:35*). His Resurrection also validates what He said about His own words:

- If you keep my commandments, you will abide in my love, just as I have kept my Father's commandments and abide in his love... You are my friends if you do what I command you. (*John 15:10, 14*)

- Heaven and earth will pass away, but my words will not pass away. (*Matthew 24:35*)

The Resurrection proved Jesus to be the indisputable authority on the Bible, which He consistently regarded as the Word of God. Therefore, we must also!

WORKS CITED

Craig, William Lane, www.leaderu.com/offices/billcraig/docs/rediscover2.html#text17.

Craig, William Lane, www.desiringgod.org/articles/historical-evidence-for-the-resurrection.

Greenleaf, Simon Dr, www://christiananswers.net/q-eden/edn-t012.html).

Kremer, Jacob, www.desiringgod.org/articles/historical-evidence-for-the-resurrection.

Lüdemann, Gerd, *"What Really Happened to Jesus?",* trans. John Bowden (Louisville, Kent: Westminster John Knox Press, 1995)

McDowell, Sean, *"Did the Apostles Really Die as Martyrs for Their Faith"*, Christian Research Journal (CRJ), Vol.39, No.2.

Strobel, Lee, *The Case for the Real Jesus*, (Grand Rapids: Zondervan, 2007)

Van Daalen, D.H., *The Real Resurrection*, (London: Collins, 1972).

Chapter 13

THE CRYPTIC OT ACCOUNTS: WHERE THE RESURRECTION IS ASSOCIATED WITH THE CRUCIFIXION

What reasons do we have to believe that the Bible is the word of God? One reason is the underlying patterns or designs found in the Hebrew Scriptures, later identified and brought to full disclosure in the New Testament.

In *"Why the Jews Rejected Jesus,"* Orthodox Jewish writer, David Klinghoffer, attempted to argue that the Jews of Jesus' day didn't have adequate reasons to believe that Jesus was their Messiah:

- If no verse in the prophets unambiguously presented resurrection as a criterion for recognizing the Messiah—and none does—then such a hypothetical wonder [Jesus' resurrection] would prove nothing. (Klinghoffer, 88)

Although Klinghoffer is correct that the Old Testament doesn't provide any *explicit* statements that the Messiah will be resurrected, there is a wealth of *implicit* evidence for the taking. *Every* Old Testament portrait of the Messiah's death is accompanied by a cryptic glimpse of His "resurrection," or at least a portrait of His life after death! If this is the case, it defies all odds and suggests that the collected books of the Hebrew Scriptures reflect a design or pattern that could only originate from above.

I'll just provide the eight clearest examples of this highly unlikely association between the Messiah's death and His return to life.

1. Peter quoted *Psalm 16* in his first evangelistic speech (*Acts 2:25-32*) in reference to Jesus' resurrection:

   • For You will not leave my [David's] soul in Sheol, nor will You allow Your Holy One to see corruption [the decay of His body] (*Psalm 16:10*).

Here, in one quick snapshot, we see the Messiah's death, but also a promise of His future life! If His body will not "see corruption," it means that it will not stay in the grave for long, unlike David's body.

2. Perhaps more dramatically, Isaiah pictures the Messiah living once again following His ordeal: (For the sake of clarity, I will now put the indications of Resurrection in CAPS.)

   • And they made His grave with the wicked--but with the rich at His death, because He had done no violence, nor was any deceit in His mouth. Yet it pleased the LORD to bruise Him; He has put Him to grief. When You make His soul an offering for sin, He SHALL SEE His seed, He SHALL PROLONG His days, and the pleasure of the LORD shall prosper in His hand. He SHALL SEE the labor of His soul, and be satisfied. By His knowledge My righteous Servant shall justify many, for He shall bear their iniquities. (*Isaiah 53:9-11*)

Although Jesus died, becoming an "offering for sin," He nevertheless "prolonged His days."

3. The Psalms provide us with a number of remarkable portraits of the crucifixion and the subsequent life of the Messiah. Although modern rabbis reject these portraits as Messianic, the Talmud, compiled around 550 AD, contains ancient rabbinic confirmation that these Psalms, to some

extent, had been regarded as Messianic (according to Alfred Edersheim, "Life and Times of Jesus the Messiah"):

- The kings of the earth set themselves, and the rulers take counsel together, against the LORD and against His Anointed, saying, "Let us break their bonds in pieces and cast away their cords from us"..."Yet I have set My King on My holy hill of Zion." "I will declare the decree: The LORD has said to Me, 'You are My Son, TODAY I HAVE BEGOTTEN YOU [from the dead; *Acts 13:33; Hebrews 1:5; 5:5*]...Kiss the Son, lest He be angry, and you perish in the way, when His wrath is kindled but a little. Blessed are all those who put their TRUST IN HIM. (*Psalm 2:2-3, 6-7, 12*)

While the fact that the Messiah lives again is explicit in this Psalm, the crucifixion is not. For this, we require the prayer uttered by Peter and John's "friends" after they were released from the Sanhedrin:

- ...through the mouth of our father David, your servant, said by the Holy Spirit, "'Why did the Gentiles rage, and the peoples plot in vain? The kings of the earth set themselves, and the rulers were gathered together, against the Lord and against his Anointed' [quoting *Psalm 2*] – for truly in this city there were gathered together against your holy servant Jesus, whom you anointed, both Herod and Pontius Pilate, along with the Gentiles and the peoples of Israel, to do whatever your hand and your plan had predestined to take place. (*Acts 4:25-28*)

According to Edersheim, the Talmud and the Midrashim also affirm this commentary regarding Psalm 2 about the suffering of the Messiah.

4. Psalm 22 provides a clearer portrait of the crucifixion, which finds ample NT support (*Matthew 27:35; Mark 15:24; John 19:24, 37*):

- For dogs have surrounded Me; the congregation of the wicked has enclosed Me. They pierced My hands and My feet; I can count all My bones. They look and stare at Me. They divide My garments among them, and for My clothing they cast lots...I WILL DECLARE YOUR NAME to My brethren; In the midst of the assembly I WILL PRAISE You. You who fear the LORD, praise Him! All you descendants of Jacob, glorify Him, and fear Him, all you offspring of Israel! For He has not despised nor abhorred the affliction of the afflicted; nor has He hidden His face from Him; but when He cried to Him, He heard. (*Psalm 22:16-18, 22-24*)

Psalm 22 also provides adequate evidence that the Messiah will live again: "nor has He hidden His face from Him; but when He cried to Him, He heard." Although the Father had temporarily (but not ultimately) turned His face from His Son, He also heard His prayer and delivered Him.

5. *Psalm 69* also receives ample NT affirmation that it provides a portrait of the crucifixion (*Matthew 27:34, 48; Luke 23:36; John 19:27*):

- Reproach has broken my heart, and I am full of heaviness; I looked for someone to take pity, but there was none; and for comforters, but I found none. They also gave me gall for my food, and for my thirst they gave me vinegar to drink...For they persecute the ones You have struck, and talk of the grief of those You have wounded...I WILL PRAISE the name of God with a song, and will MAGNIFY HIM with thanksgiving. This also shall please the LORD better than an ox or bull, which has horns and hooves. The humble shall see this and be glad; and you who seek God, your hearts shall live. (*Psalm 69:20-21; 26, 30-32*)

Once again, we find evidence here that the crucified Messiah lives again. Subsequent to His ordeal, "He will praise the name of God" and "magnify Him." However, both *Psalms 69* and *40* do not receive Talmudic affirmation that they are Messianic.

6. Nevertheless, *Psalm 40* reveals that animal sacrifice will be replaced by the ultimate sacrifice to which the animal sacrifices pointed:

   - *Psalm 40:6-10* "Sacrifice and offering You did not desire; my ears You have opened. ("A body Thou hast prepared for Me." LXX; *Hebrews 10:5*) Burnt offering and sin offering You did not require. Then I said, "Behold, I come; in the scroll of the book it is written of me. I delight to do Your will, O my God, and Your law is within my heart." I HAVE PROCLAIMED THE GOOD NEWS OF RIGHTEOUSNESS in the great assembly; indeed, I do not restrain my lips, O LORD, You Yourself know. I have not hidden Your righteousness within my heart; I HAVE DECLARED YOUR FAITHFULNESS AND YOUR SALVATION; I HAVE NOT CONCEALED Your lovingkindness and Your truth from the great assembly.

Although these references to the presence of the Messiah after His death are cryptic, they are still blatantly present and accompany *each* reference to the death of the Messiah.

7. *Zechariah* is even more cryptic but also revealing of the Trinity:

   - And I will pour on the house of David and on the inhabitants of Jerusalem the Spirit of grace and supplication; THEN THEY WILL LOOK ON **ME** WHOM THEY PIERCED. Yes, they will mourn for **Him** as one mourns for his only son, and grieve for Him as one grieves for a firstborn"… And one will say to him, "What are these wounds between your arms?" Then he will answer, "Those with which I was wounded in the house of my friends." "Awake, O sword, against My Shepherd, against the Man who is My companion," Says the LORD of hosts. "Strike the Shepherd, and the sheep will be scattered." (*Zechariah 12:10; 13:6-7*). Jesus had quoted this final phrase to prepare His disciples for their betrayal of their Master. (*Matthew 26:31; Mark 14:27*)

In this passage, God reveals that the Messiah will be pierced. The "sword" will come against Him. As a result, once Israel's eyes have been opened, they will mourn for the One they had killed. However, God also reveals that it is *He, the One who now speaks* to Israel, who has been pierced to death. Thus, He reveals that there is a distinction in the Godhead, because they will mourn for *Him,* not just for *ME* (the One who is speaking)!

8. This prophecy from Daniel is equally cryptic about the fact that the Messiah will live again:

- *Daniel 9:24-26* "Seventy weeks are determined for your people and for your holy city, to finish the transgression, to make an end of sins, to make reconciliation ["atonement" in the KJV] for iniquity, to bring in everlasting righteousness, to seal up vision and prophecy, and TO ANOINT THE MOST HOLY. Know therefore and understand, that from the going forth of the command to restore and build Jerusalem until Messiah the Prince [comes; week 69] there shall be seven weeks and sixty-two weeks; the street shall be built again, and the wall, even in troublesome times.

141

And after the sixty-two weeks Messiah shall be cut off, but not for Himself; and the people of the prince who is to come shall destroy the city and the sanctuary. The end of it shall be with a flood, and till the end of the war desolations are determined.

Notice several curiosities – the Messiah is "cut off" (killed) in week 62 but is anointed afterwards in week 70, after His death. Also note that the Messiah will return in week 69, once again after being "cut off."

I also want to briefly cite two additional cryptic hints or allusions to the crucifixion and the Messiah's life afterwards:

- Into Your hand I commit my spirit (*Luke 23:46*) affirms that this refers to the crucifixion]; You have redeemed me, O LORD God of truth. (*Psalm 31:5*)

- He guards all his bones; not one of them is broken (*John 19:36; Exodus 12:46*) ...The LORD redeems the soul of His servants, and none of those who trust in Him shall be condemned. (*Psalm 34:20, 22*)

Admittedly, all of these references are cryptic. Because of this, many have mistakenly charged that the resurrection is a New Testament addition or invention:

- Resurrection of the dead, it is argued, is a Johnny-come-lately notion, not found in the ancient texts of the Hebrew Bible, which treated mortality matter-of-factly. Instead the doctrine was an innovation of the Maccabean period...when faithful Jews were being persecuted by the Hellenistic monarch Antiochus IV. With ideas borrowed from Zoroastrianism and other foreign sources, resurrection solved the puzzle of understanding divine justice when fidelity to the Law brought about not prosperity and length of years by martyrdom (Steinfels, NYT).

I hope that these various prophecies from the Hebrew Scriptures have answered this false charge. However, you are probably left with a perplexing question:

- If the crucifixion and the resurrection are so central to God's plan, as clearly revealed in the New Testament, why did our Lord so diligently hide His plan?

Perhaps Paul provides the best explanation:

- But we speak the wisdom of God in a mystery, the hidden wisdom which God ordained before the ages for our glory, which none of the rulers of this age knew; for had they known, **they would not have crucified the Lord of glory** (*1 Corinthians2:7-8*; emphasis mine).

What does all of this tell us about the nature of Scripture? How do we explain this consistent but consistently cryptic design that we find throughout the various books of the Hebrew Scriptures? Why do we not find just one indication of the crucifixion without an accompanying assurance that He will return?

This couldn't have been the result of a collaborative human effort. If humans had invented this message, they would have presented it clearly. What would be the sense of promoting a message that no one would even notice?

Of course, the same objection can be brought against God's authorship. Why would He hide away such a central disclosure? Peter explained that the Prophets of Israel didn't fully understand what they had been given to write. Instead, it was revealed to them that what they had written was for future generations – for us!

- Concerning this salvation, the prophets who prophesied about the grace that was to be yours searched and inquired carefully, inquiring what person or time the Spirit of Christ in them was indicating when he predicted the sufferings of Christ and the subsequent glories. It was revealed to them that they were serving not themselves but you, in the things that have now been announced to you through those who preached the good news to you by the Holy Spirit sent from heaven, things into which angels long to look. (*1 Peter 1:10-12*)

I thank God for His various hidden revelations. This skeptic continues to find great assurance and courage by feeding upon such jewels.

WORKS CITED

Edersheim, Alfred, *The Life and Times of Jesus the Messiah*, (McClean, VA: Macdonald Publishing, no publication date given)

Klinghoffer, David, *Why the Jews Rejected Jesus,* (New York: Doubleday, First Edition, 2005)

Steinfels, Peter, New York Times, 9/30/06

Chapter 14

EXTERNAL CONFIRMATIONS OF SCRIPTURE

Is the Bible's reliability and historicity supported by evidence external to the Bible?

This is a huge question, which calls upon every area of human inquiry to pass judgment. Do the fields of history, archeology, geology, psychology, linguistics, astronomy, sociology, and physics validate or invalidate the biblical accounts?

More specifically, "Does the composite NT Greek text, derived from the almost 6000 ancient Greek manuscripts and fragments closely approximate what the original writings must have looked like?" New Testament scholars, historians, and archeologists give high grades to the composite New Testament Greek text. Based upon the textual evidence, even the agnostic New Testament Critic, Bart Ehrman, confessed:

- The oldest and best sources we have for knowing about the life of Jesus…are the four Gospels of the NT…This is not simply the view of Christian historians who have a high opinion of the NT and in its historical worth; it is the view of all serious historians of antiquity…it is the conclusion that has been reached by every one of the hundreds (thousands, even) of scholars. (Ehrman, *Misquoting Jesus*, 102)

Ehrman, who likes to impugn the many NT texts, had been asked:

- Bruce Metzger [the leading textual credit of his day] your mentor in textual criticism to whom this book ["Misquoting Jesus"] is dedicated, has said that there is nothing in these variants of Scripture that challenges any essential Christian beliefs…Why do you believe these core tenants of Christian orthodoxy to be in jeopardy based on the scribal errors you discovered in the biblical manuscripts? (Ibid., 252)

Ehrman answered:

- Even though we may disagree on important religious questions – he is a formally committed Christian and I am not – we are in complete agreement on a number of very important historical and textual questions. If he and I were put in a room and asked to hammer out a consensus statement on what we think the original text of the New Testament probably looked like, there would be very few points of disagreement…The position I argue for in *Misquoting Jesus* does not actually stand at odds with Prof. Metzger's position that the essential Christian beliefs are not affected by the textual variants in the manuscript tradition of the New Testament. (Ibid., 252)

Metzger had claimed the text of the NT to be "99.5 free from textual discrepancies." Ehrman, ordinarily the strongest disparaging voice regarding the certainty of the Biblical text, also admitted:

- The more manuscripts one discovers, the more the variant readings; but also the more the likelihood that somewhere among those variants readings one will be able to uncover the original text. Therefore, the thirty thousand variants uncovered by [critic John] Mill do not detract from the integrity of the New Testament; they simply provide the data scholars need to work on to establish the text, a text that is more amply documented than any other in the ancient world. (Ehrman, *Misquoting Truth*, 87)

There is a strong consensus among NT textual critics that from the almost 6,000 ancient Greek manuscripts and fragments, the original text can be very closely approximated. In *Misquoting Truth*, Timothy Paul Jones adds:

- Sir Frederic Kenyon, former director of the British Museum, once commented concerning the Gospels, "The interval between the dates of the original compositions and the earliest extant [existing manuscripts] evidence [is] so small as to be negligible, and the last foundation for any doubt that the Scriptures have come down to us substantially as they were written has now been removed." (Ehrman, *Misquoting Truth*, 50)

NT scholar William Warren concurs:

- I would say that our [present composite NT] text almost certainly represents a form that is almost identical to the original documents. (Ehrman/Wallace, *The Reliability of the NT*, 122)

Another NT scholar, Craig Evans, affirms the same thing:

- Given the evidence, we have every reason to have confidence in the text of Scripture. This does not mean that we possess 100% certainty that we have the exact wording in every case, but we have good reason to believe that what we have preserved in the several hundred manuscripts of the first millennium is the text that the writers of Scripture penned.

Similarly, NT textual critic Silvie Raquel writes:

- I also have studied New Testament textual criticism and, by contrast with Ehrman, have found confirmation about the validity of the text...by defective reasoning, misuse of the evidence, and a misconception of inerrancy, Ehrman fails to build a case for the unreliability of the New Testament text as a sacred and inspired text. (Ehrman/Wallace, *The Reliability of the NT*, 173, 185)

Daniel Wallace concluded:

- On the contrary, it [scholarship] has built it [my faith]. I've asked questions all my life, I've dug into the text, I've studied this thoroughly, and today I know with confidence that my trust in Jesus has been well placed...very well placed.

Greek scholar D.A. Carson sums up the evidence this way:

The purity of text is of such a substantial nature that nothing we believe to be true, and nothing we are commanded to do, is in any way jeopardized by the variants.

And what about the historical accuracy of the Gospels? About Luke, New Testament scholar, F.F.Bruce, has written:

- A man whose accuracy can be demonstrated in matters where we are able to test it is likely to be accurate even where means of testing aren't available. Accuracy is a habit of mind...Luke's record entitles him to be regarded as a writer of habitual accuracy.

Archeologist John McRay adds:

- One prominent archeologist carefully examined Luke's references to 32 countries, 54 cities, and 9 Islands w/o finding a single mistake. (Strobel, *Case For Christ,* 125-145*)*

About the *Gospel of John*, McRay claims:

- It [the Pool of Bethesda] lies maybe 40 feet below ground – and sure enough, there are five porticoes...exactly as John had described. And you have other discoveries – the Pool of Siloam from *John 9:7*, Jacob's Well from *John 4:12*, the probable location of the Stone Pavement near the Jaffa gate where Jesus appeared before Pontius Pilate in *John 19:13*, even Pilate's own identity – all of which have lent credibility to John's Gospel. (Strobel, 125-145)

- Archeology has not produced anything that is unequivocally a contradiction to the Bible. On the contrary, as we've seen, there have been many opinions of skeptical scholars that have become codified into 'fact' over the years, but that archeology has shown to be wrong.

In fact, the textual evidence along with other forms of historical evidence are so compelling that even skeptics acknowledge that the Apostles had been convinced that they had encountered the resurrected Jesus, as I have detailed in the chapter on the Resurrection.

Even the atheist Ludemann had conceded:

- It may be taken as historically certain that Peter and the disciples had experiences after Jesus' death in which Jesus appeared to them as the risen Christ. (Strobel, *The Case for Faith,* 83)

Jewish NT scholar Paula Fredriksen also conceded:

- The Disciples' conviction that they had seen the risen Christ...is historical bedrock, facts known past doubting. (Strobel)

149

NT scholar James Dunn went a step further:

- It is an undoubted fact that the conviction that God had raised Jesus from the dead and had exalted Jesus to his right hand transformed Jesus' first disciples and their beliefs about Jesus. (McDowell, CRJ)

All the above represent affirmations of the Christian faith based historical and textual evidences. However, there are many other forms of external confirmations.

Do scientific findings confirm the Bible? Atheist Sam Harris denies that it does:

- [The Bible] does not contain a single sentence that could not have been written by a man or a woman living in the first century. (www:samharris.org)

On the contrary, it seems that the Bible had anticipated many of the findings of modern science:

1. TIME IS NOT ETERNAL: who has saved us and called us to a holy life--not because of anything we have done but because of his own purpose and grace. This grace was given us in Christ Jesus before the beginning of time, (2 Timothy 1:9)

2. THE UNIVERSE HAD A BEGINNING: In the beginning God created the heavens and the earth. (Contra the steady-state theory that had ruled science). (Genesis 1:1).

3. THE BUILDING BLOCKS OF THE PHYSICAL WORD AREN'T VISIBLE: By faith we understand that the universe was formed at God's command, so that what is seen was not made out of what was visible. (Hebrews 11:3)

4. ONE LAND MASS: And God said, Let the waters under the heavens be gathered together into one place, and let the dry land appear. And it was so. (This conforms to the present theory that the continents had drifted apart.) (*Genesis 1:9*)

5. GENETICS SHOW THAT WE ALL CAME FROM A SINGLE SET OF PARENTS: And he made from one man every nation of mankind to live on all the face of the earth, having determined allotted periods and the boundaries of their dwelling place. (*Acts 17:26*)

6. WATER CYCLE: He draws up the drops of water, which distill as rain to the streams. (*Job 36:27*. Also *Amos 9:6*)

7. THE EXISTENCE OF DINOSAURS: It was you who crushed the heads of Leviathan and gave him as food to the creatures of the desert. (*Psalm 74:14*)

8. STARS AS GUIDES TO SEASONS AND GEOGRAPHIC POSITIONS: Lights in the expanse of the sky... [would] serve as signs to mark seasons and days and years. (*Genesis 1:14*)

9. GOD WORKS THROUGH FIXED LAWS: *Jeremiah 33:25* states that God accomplishes His purposes through "fixed laws of heaven and earth." (Although science *demonstrated* that phenomena operated according to laws, the Bible long before posited the operation of the God's laws.) (Also *Job 38:33*)

10. COUNTLESS STARS: I will make the descendants of David my servant and the Levites who minister before me as <u>countless</u> as the stars of the sky and as measureless as the sand on the seashore. (*Jeremiah 33:22. Also Job 11:7-8; 22:12*)

11. ROUND EARTH, EXPANDING UNIVERSE: He sits enthroned above the <u>circle</u> of the earth, and its people are like grasshoppers. He <u>stretches out</u> the heavens like a canopy, and spreads them out like a tent to live in (*Isaiah 40:22; 42:5*).

12. THE EARTH DOES NOT SIT ON A PEDESTAL AS ANE COSMOLOGY HAS IT: He spreads out the northern skies over empty space; he suspends the earth over nothing. (*Job 26:7*)

13. STRESS NEGATIVELY IMPACTS HEALTH: A cheerful heart is good medicine, but a crushed spirit dries up the bones. (*Proverbs 17:22*)

14. UNHEALTHY QUALITY OF EXCREMENT: Designate a place outside the camp where you can go to relieve yourself. As part of your equipment have something to dig with, and when you relieve yourself, dig a hole and cover up your excrement. (*Deuteronomy 23:12-13*)

15. FOSSIL FINDS IN THE MOUNTAINS: …the waters stood above the mountains. (Even Everest), (*Psalm 104:6*)

Don't be too impressed with this kind of evidence. Why not? It is only impressive in light of the findings of modern-day science, which seem to be in constant flux. However, this evidence serves as a powerful rebuttal to Bible-detractors who argue that the Bible fails to accord with our present-day scientific consensus and is therefore wrong. Generally, as science begins to uncover the increasing complexity and marvel of creation, the Biblical doctrine of Intelligent Design is further validated, while naturalistic theories have been debunked. Consequently, no one is talking about vestigial organs (leftovers from primate "ancestors") or junk DNA. Why not? We have found that all of these have their function, supporting the design hypothesis.

In fact, we observe evidences of design wherever we look. Nobel Prize winner in Physics, Arno Penzias, observed:

- Astronomy leads us to a unique event, a universe which was created out of nothing, one with the very delicate balance needed to provide exactly the conditions required to permit life, and one which has an underlying (one might say 'supernatural') plan.

We can even point to psychology for confirmation of the Biblical worldview. Psychologists now recognize the very same elements needed for human thriving that the Bible has taught too two thousand years ago – other-centeredness, love, forgiveness, confession, truth, gratitude, living according to our conscience, and even trust in a benign Higher Power. Consequently, surveys have shown that Christians tend to be healthier both psychologically and physically.

I have just touched upon a small sample of the various ways that the Bible receives external confirmation from the surrounding physical world. Along with science, history, and textual studies, psychology, sociology, philosophy, and ethics can also be consulted in this regard.

Consequently, we can spend more than an entire lifetime exploring this almost limitless subject. However, we have to be careful that our estimation of Scripture doesn't rise and fall according to the most recent touted theories of these various disciplines. Instead, the Bible requires that all forms of knowledge must be judged by the Scriptures (*2 Corinthians 10:4-5; Isaiah 8:19-20; 1 Corinthians 4:6-7; 1 Peter 4:11*).

WORKS CITED

Ehrman, Bart D., *Truth and Fiction in the Da Vinci Code: A Historian Reveals What We Really Know About Jesus, Mary Magdlene and Constantine"*, (NY: Oxford University Press, 2006}.

Ehrman, Bart D., *Misquoting Jesus*: *The Story Who Changed the Bible and Why,* (NY: HarperOne, 2005)

Ehrman, Bart and Wallace, Daniel, *The Reliability of the New Testament: Bart D. Ehrman and Daniel B. Wallace in Dialogue, co-authored with Bart Ehrman and Robert Stewart* (Minneapolis: Fortress, 2010)

Harris, Sam, www.samharris.org/reply-to-a-christian/

McDowell, Sean, *"Did the Apostles Really Die as Martyrs for Their Faith",* Christian Research Journal (CRJ), Vol.39, No.2.

Strobel, Lee, *The Case for Christ*: *A Journalist's Personal Investigation of the Evidence for Jesus*, (Grand Rapids: Zondervan, 1998)

Strobel, Lee, *The Case For Faith: A Journalist Investigates the Toughest Objections to Christianity,* (Grand Rapids: Zondervan, 2000)

Chapter 15

ENEMY TESTIMONY AND HOW IT SERVES TO AUTHENTICATE THE NEW TESTAMENT

Testimony offered against the interests of the testifier is as highly regarded as deathbed confessions. In contrast, Bill Clinton's autobiography had been panned by the critics because his testimony was deemed to be self-serving. He only confessed what everyone already knew – his affair with Monica Lewinsky.

Likewise, it is expected that Orthodox Jews will justify their rejection of Jesus. However, when they admit the existence of evidence contrary to their position, this evidence carries more weight than if this disclosure had supported their position. Let's look at several interesting instances of this.

In *"Why the Jews Rejected Jesus,"* Orthodox Jewish scholar, David Klinghoffer, admitted:

- The Talmud states that from forty years before the Temple's destruction and onward, there were supernatural omens of the disaster to come--that is, starting from the inception of the Christian religion following the death of Jesus. The eternal fire of the Temple altar would not stay lit. The monumental bronze Temple gates opened by themselves. Josephus confirms the Talmud's account of the inner Sanctuary's east gate and its mysterious openings. He adds other portents from these years: a bright light shining around the altar and the Sanctuary at three in the morning, a cow brought for sacrifice giving birth to a lamb, apparitions of chariots and armies flying through the sky above the whole land of Israel. (Klinghoffer 117)

The openings of the "inner Sanctuary's east gate" would have been interpreted by the Jews of Jesus' day to mean that God was vacating His Sanctuary, leaving it defenseless (*Ezekiel 8:6, 18-19*). "The eternal fire of the Temple" that wouldn't stay lit conveyed a similar message. It was supposed to always be burning (*Exodus 27:20*) and represented the presence of God (*1 Samuel 1:3*). The fact that it wouldn't stay lit seemingly represented God's sign that He was leaving the Temple to its destruction. Of course, the apparitions in the sky represented the returning Roman army.

The *Jerusalem Talmud* substantiates the above account taken from the Babylonian Talmud:

- 'Said Rabban Yohanan Ben Zakkai to the Temple, 'O Temple, why do you frighten us? We know that you will end up destroyed. For it has been said, 'Open your doors, O Lebanon, that the fire may devour your cedars.' (*Sota 6:3*)

- Forty years before the destruction of the Temple, the western light went out, the crimson thread remained crimson, and the lot for the Lord always came up in the left hand. They would close the gates of the Temple by night and get up in the morning and find them wide open. (Neusner, 156-157)

Amazingly, after the Crucifixion (circa. 30 AD) and for the next 40 years until the destruction of the Temple in 70 AD, Israel had been drenched by a series of miraculous omens pointing ominously to their future destruction.

Earnest Martin has commented about the Temple lamps:

- 'In fact, we are told in the Talmud that at dusk the lamps that were unlit in the daytime (the middle four lamps remained unlit, while the two eastern lamps normally stayed lit during the day) were to be re-lit from the flames of the western lamp (which was a lamp that was supposed to stay lit all the time — it was like the 'eternal' flame that we see today in some national monuments) . . .

- 'This 'western lamp' was to be kept lit at all times. For that reason, the priests kept extra reservoirs of olive oil and other implements in ready supply to make sure that the 'western lamp' (under all circumstances) would stay lit. But what happened in the forty years from the very year Messiah said the physical Temple would be destroyed? Every night for forty years the western lamp went out, and this in spite of the priests each evening preparing in a special way the western lamp so that it would remain constantly burning all night!' (Martin, Ernest, 4).

Why would Jewish sources trying to debunk Christianity make such an incredible admission? Klinghoffer tried to interpret the miraculous events as omens directed against the Jewish believers in Christ: "*Was God not warning the people of the disastrous course some [the Jewish Christians] had set out upon?*"

However, the Christians had fled to safety across the Jordan to Pella! According to Klinghoffer, it was the Christians who should have been penalized for their heresy. However, it was the Jews who didn't believe in Christ, who were left to pay the price.

What is even more unbelievable about Klinghoffer's explanation is the timing of the omens. They began, according to Klinghoffer, at approximately the time of the Crucifixion (30 AD) and lasted for forty years until the destruction of the Temple. They therefore served as a warning to those who had crucified Jesus to repent, not to those who had followed Jesus.

And when did the omens end? After the great slaughter of the Jews and destruction of their Temple! This had nothing to do with any divine displeasure with the Jewish believers in Christ. Had the omens been sent because of God's displeasure with Jesus, they would have ended at the Cross. However, it was at *this time* that the omens of doom began, presumably because Israel had rejected their Messiah and then refused to repent.

Klinghoffer asserts that the warnings were directed towards the Jewish Christians who had gone astray. However, if this had been the case, calamity should have fallen on them. Instead, it fell upon the nation of Israel. Why? Israel had refused to repent of their sins and seek God's mercy, as Jesus had warned:

- O Jerusalem, Jerusalem, you who kill the prophets and stone those sent to you, how often I have longed to gather your children together, as a hen gathers her chicks under her wings, but you were not willing. Look, your house is left to you desolate. (*Matthew 23:37-38*)

Another interesting example comes from the Talmud. For many years prior to the Cross, during the celebration of the Day of Atonement (Yom Kippur), the sins of Israel were confessed upon the head of the Scapegoat who was then lead away into the wilderness, symbolizing the fact that God had taken away Israel's sins.

However, this ritual was attended by a great miracle. A red died woolen skin was attached to the head of the Scapegoat, which miraculously would turn white in front of the great masses of Israel. They understood that this symbolized the fact that God had removed their sins. (*Isaiah 1:18*).

In his response to the question, "Why didn't the red ribbon on the head of the Scapegoat [on Yom Kippur] turn white in 30 AD?" Jewish anti-Christian apologist, Rabbi Tovia Singer, reluctantly admits:

> "In *Tractate Yoma 39b*, the Talmud... discusses numerous remarkable phenomena that occurred in the Temple during the Yom Kippur service... There was a strip of scarlet-dyed wool tied to the head of the scapegoat which would turn white in the presence of the large crowd gathered at the Temple on the Day of Atonement. The Jewish people perceived this miraculous transformation as a heavenly sign that their sins were forgiven. The Talmud relates, however, that 40 years before the destruction of the second Temple [approximately 30 AD at the time of the Crucifixion] the scarlet colored strip of wool did not turn white. (Singer, Talmud 39b)

This is a damning admission. Following the Crucifixion, the scarlet wool would no longer miraculously become white! It seems that God had put Israel on notice that He would no longer accept animal sacrifices now that the ultimate offering of Jesus had been accomplished.

How does Singer explain this cessation at the very time of the Cross? He claims that various miracles were gradually disappearing because Israel's "dedication to the golden rule slacked off." However, the timing of this cessation couldn't have been worse for the Jews who had rejected their one Hope, even in the light of so many miraculous signs that had validated the Person of Jesus.

Singer also insists that God had been angry with Jesus for deceiving Israel. However, if so, we'd have expected Him to grant signs of His approval of the Crucifixion, instead of a sign of disapproval — that He no longer honored the scapegoat to take away Israel's sins. God's timing couldn't have been worse for Singer!

One Final Example: Did Jesus perform many miracles? If so, the miracles would validate His claims, and His detractors would have to offer alternative explanations or deny them altogether. However, they did not deny His miracles but instead ascribed them to black magic and Satan (*Matthew 12*). This is exactly what we find in many of the Talmudic writings:

- *Shabbath 104b*, p.504 "Jesus was a MAGICIAN and a fool. Mary was an adulteress".

- *Sanhedrin 107B* of the Babylonian Talmud: "Jesus... stood up a brick to symbolize an idol and bowed down to it. Jesus performed MAGIC and incited the people of Israel and led them astray."

- *Sanhedrin 43A*: "On Passover Eve they hanged Jesus of Nazareth. He practiced SORCERY, incited and led Israel astray...Was Jesus of Nazareth deserving of a search for an argument in his favor? He was an enticer and the Torah says, 'You shall not spare, nor shall you conceal him!"

Josephus, (*Antiquities* (90 AD), XVIII 3.2):

- About this time arose Jesus, a wise man, who did good deeds and whose virtues were recognized. And many Jews and people of other nations became his disciples. Pilate condemned him to be crucified and to die. However, those who became his disciples preached his doctrine. They related that he had appeared to them three days after his crucifixion and that he was alive. Perhaps he was the Messiah in connection with whom the prophets foretold WONDERS.

According to *The Jewish Encyclopedia*, Jesus was often accused by the Talmudists of performing magic:

- It is the tendency of all these sources to belittle the person of Jesus by ascribing to him illegitimate birth, MAGIC, and a shameful death …

- Magic may have been ascribed him over against the miracles recorded in the Gospels.

- Toledot Jesu": "When Jesus was expelled from the circle of scholars, he is said to have returned secretly from Galilee to Jerusalem, where he inserted a parchment containing the "declared name of God" ("Shem ha-Meforash"), which was guarded in the Temple, into his skin, carried it away, and then, taking it out of his skin, he performed his MIRACLES by its means. This magic formula then had to be recovered from him, and Judah the Gardener (a personage of the "Toledot" corresponding to Judas Iscariot) offered to do it; he and Jesus then engaged in an aerial battle (borrowed from the legend of SIMON MAGUS), in which Judah remained victor and Jesus fled.

While these sources (except for Josephus) demean Jesus, they still acknowledge that He had performed miracles. This is remarkable, because it would have been easier to deny that the miracles had ever taken place. Evidently, they were not able to do this without being derided by the many who knew that He was a miracle worker.

But could He have been evil and used black magic, as the Jewish sources allege? Evidently, if they could have proved this allegation, their trial of Jesus would have been easy. However, they were unable to find witnesses to validate their claims.

His miracles not only stand as facts, but they also testify in favor of His teachings and the New Testament claims.

WORKS CITED

The Jewish Encyclopedia,
www.come-and-hear.com/editor/censorship_2.html

Josephus, (Antiquities (90 AD), XVIII 3.2)

Klinghoffer, David, *Why the Jews Rejected Jesus,* (New York: Doubleday, First Edition, 2005)

Martin, Ernest*, The Significance of the Year CE 30, Research Update,* April 1994.

Neusner, Jacob, "*The Yerushalmi - The Talmud of the Land of Israel: An Introduction*", Jason Aronson, 1994)

Singer, Tovia, Tractate *Yoma 39b, the Talmud*.

Chapter 16

IF SCRIPTURE DOES CHANGE, SHOULD WE NOT BE UNDER THE MOSAIC COVENANT AS THE RABBIS CLAIM?

In these final chapters, I am trying to prove that the Bible can prove that it comes from God. However, skeptics often scoff, "Something cannot prove itself."

However, the Bible is a collection of 66 Books. I also refer them to the phenomenon of life itself. Its overwhelming complexity, functionality, harmony, and design point to an Intelligent Designer. How? For one thing, life defies a natural explanation. For another thing, life is clearly the product of intelligent design as a book or a computer program is a product of design. I hope to demonstrate that the Bible is also the product of intelligent design, and that its internal consistency argues in favor of one magnificent intelligent Designer.

The Bible was written by many different authors from various cultures, time periods, and languages, over a period of perhaps 1500 years. We should expect that they would reflect theologies at variance with each other. We should also expect that the rabbis would have a better understanding of the Hebrew Scriptures than does the New Testament, since they claim to be more in touch with the language and culture of the Hebrew Scriptures.

However, the entirety of the Bible – both the OT and the NT – demonstrates an astonishing degree of theological consistency. Of course, this assertion requires a massive amount of argumentation and evidential support. Therefore, for the sake of simplicity, let's confine the argument to a single contentious issue.

Orthodox Jewish authorities commonly insist that God's Word (the Hebrew Scriptures) doesn't change. However, the New Testament represents an unwarranted change:

- The New Testament misinterprets our Hebrew Scriptures. It misrepresents the Mosaic covenant as the source of death (*James 2:10; Romans7:9; 3:20; 2 Corinthians3:6*) and claims that it will pass away! On the contrary, the Mosaic Covenant imparts life (*Psalm1; 119:32, 92, 104,127,144*), and the Word of God doesn't change! (*Isa.40:8*)

This is a common and formidable rabbinic challenge. However, there are many indications within the Hebrew Scriptures that the Mosaic Covenant was temporary. Jeremiah wrote that the Mosaic Covenant would come to an end with the advent of a New Covenant:

- Behold, the days are coming, says the Lord, when I will make a new covenant with the house of Israel and with the house of Judah—not according to the covenant that I made with their fathers in the day that I took them by the hand to lead them out of the land of Egypt, My covenant which they broke. (*Jeremiah 31:31–32; Hebrews 8:8–9*)

Doesn't this settle the matter? Hasn't the "New Covenant" superseded the old? Not according to rabbinic scholar Gerald Sigal:

- By any objective reading of the text, one fails to see any reference to a substitution of a new covenant which will supersede the old. There is nothing in Jeremiah's statement to suggest that the new covenant will contain any changes in the Law (the Mosaic Covenant). (Sigal, 70)

Jeremiah, however, wrote that God would establish a "new covenant." Therefore, wasn't it intended to replace the Mosaic covenant, which Israel continued to break? Not according to Sigal:

- Obviously, Jeremiah's 'new covenant' is not to be viewed as a replacement of the existing (Mosaic) covenant, but merely as a figure of speech for the reinvigoration and revitalization of the old (Mosaic) covenant. (Sigal, 73)

According to Sigal, the New Covenant is the Mosaic Covenant with a minor face-lift. Jeremiah, however, claims that this "new covenant" will *not* resemble the old (*Jeremiah 31:32*). Why not? Because the Mosaic Covenant was a failure, at least in the sense that Israel failed to keep it. Israel "broke" it as naturally as breathing. It had to be replaced by something new. (Evangelical scholars debate over the nature of the covenants (e.g., whether the Abrahamic covenant is conditional or unconditional and the relationship between them (e.g., whether the Mosaic covenant is unique or whether it is fundamentally a reiteration of previous covenants).

When we examine the features of the New Covenant further, we find that they represent more than a face-lift, but rather, a major overhaul. There are laws in it, but they are also inscribed on the heart. Also forgiveness is both thorough and permanent, whereas under the Mosaic scheme, sacrificial offerings had to be made on a continual basis for the sins of the people.

Sigal defends his interpretation by citing *Psalm 111:7–8* and *Isaiah 40:8*, which state that God's Word doesn't change (Sigal, 72). A change in covenants, however, doesn't imply that God's Word had changed or had been wrong. It simply implies that a new time and situation demands a new course of action – the New Covenant.

165

For example, when Israel crossed the Jordan into the Promised Land, God's *activity* changed—the manna ceased falling—but God's Word hadn't changed. He never promised that manna would always fall from heaven.

Sigal's other defense is more to the point:

- That the covenant of old is of eternal duration, never to be rescinded or to be superseded by a new covenant, is clearly stated in Leviticus 26:44–45. (Sigal, 71)

If Sigal is correct, these verses offer clear support for his contention that the Mosaic Covenant can never be superseded, and he then might be justified in his awkward interpretation of Jeremiah. These verses read:

- "Yet for all that, when they are in the land of their enemies, I will not cast them away, nor shall I abhor them, to utterly destroy them and break My covenant with them; for I am the Lord their God. But for their sake I will remember the covenant of their ancestors, whom I brought out of the land of Egypt in the sight of the nations, that I might be their God: I am the Lord." (*Leviticus 26:44–45*)

Is this "covenant of their ancestors" the Mosaic Covenant? No. In the preceding two verses in Leviticus, the Lord identifies the covenant to which He refers: "Then I will remember my covenant with Jacob, and my covenant with Isaac and my covenant with Abraham I will remember…they will accept their guilt, because they despised My judgments and because their soul abhorred My statutes." (*Leviticus 26:42–43*)

It's because of God's unchanging, unconditional promises to the patriarchs that Israel had hope, not because of the Mosaic Covenant that brought condemnation to Israel according to her deeds. This was the prime purpose for the highly conditional Mosaic Covenant: to show Israel in neon lights the extent of her damning sins, and thereby to impress on her the need for a Savior and to lead her to grace. (*Romans3:19–20; Galatians3:22–24*)

Nevertheless, at first blush, "the covenant of their ancestors, whom I brought out of the land of Egypt" (v.45) could understandably be mistaken for the Mosaic covenant. This apparent contradiction between vv.42-43 and v.45 is easily resolved, however, once we remember that the Abrahamic Covenant had been renewed with Isaac, then with Jacob and his sons and hence with all Israel; consequently, while it is true that Israel had been under the Mosaic, they were no less under the Abrahamic.

An additional reason to understand Moses as referring to the Abrahamic Covenant is that at the time that Israel was "brought out of the land of Egypt," they were only under the Abrahamic. The installation of the Mosaic covenant had to wait for an additional two months.

How could Sigal have made such a mistake? Weren't there other verses to which he could have appealed to make his case that the Mosaic covenant was everlasting? If so, he doesn't seem to be aware of them. Is there any evidence that the Mosaic is everlasting and therefore won't be replaced?

THE MOSAIC COVENANT WAS TEMPORARY

Jeremiah prophesied that God would make a "new covenant" unlike the old one. The old, however, would not remain side-by-side with the new. "'Then it shall come to pass, when you are multiplied and increased in the land in those days,' says the Lord, 'that they will say no more, "The ark of the covenant of the Lord." It shall not come to mind, nor shall they remember it, nor shall they visit it, nor shall it be made anymore.'" (*Jeremiah 3:16*, emphases added; see also *Isaiah 43:18; 65:17*)

The "ark of the covenant" represented the Mosaic covenant. It was the receptacle for the two tablets of the Ten Commandments, the centerpiece of the Mosaic institution. When Jeremiah said that the "ark of the covenant" will "not come to mind," he was symbolically referring to the Mosaic covenant. It would not come to mind because it would be replaced by another system that would "feed [them] with knowledge and understanding" (*Jeremiah 3:15*). If the Mosaic covenant would not be remembered, then it would certainly not be in effect.

The Mosaic was not merely limited in duration; it was also limited in location to the Promised Land. Moses reminded Israel: "You shall not at all do as we are doing here today— every man doing whatever is right in his own eyes—for as yet you have NOT COME TO THE REST and the inheritance which the Lord your God is giving you" (*Deuteronomy 12:8–9*).

Israel was free from many of the legal stipulations as long as it had not yet reached the Promised Land. The fact that the Israelites born during the desert wandering had not been circumcised provides strong evidence of this (*Joshua 5:5*).

The Mosaic Covenant was never called "everlasting." This wasn't because Scripture seldom describes covenants in general as everlasting. On the contrary, many covenants are so referenced; but never the Mosaic. The first covenant mentioned in the Bible is the one that was made with Noah (*Genesis 9:16; Isaiah 54:9–10*) and it was called "everlasting."

The next covenant was that made with Abraham and subsequently extended to Isaac and Jacob. This too was termed an "everlasting" covenant (*Genesis 17:19,13; Psalm 105:9–10,42; 1 Chronicles 16:15–17*). (How can these covenants be everlasting in light of the fact that the New is the everlasting covenant? The promises of these covenants will be carried over into the New, where they will find their ultimate fulfillment).

The Mosaic Covenant was next. This one formed the center of Israelite thought and practice and had center stage throughout the bulk of the Hebrew Scriptures. The Scriptures, however, never referred to it as "everlasting" or "eternal" or by any other term to that effect. (*Isaiah 24:5* makes mention of an "everlasting covenant" that can easily be mistaken as the Mosaic; however, the context suggests that this covenant applies to all humankind.) The absence of any such description is profoundly significant given the Covenant's prominent place in Israelite life.

The next covenant was a "perpetual" covenant given within the framework of the Mosaic: the Sabbath (*Exodus 31:16-17*). The perpetuity of the Sabbath, however, doesn't suggest that the Mosaic Covenant was also perpetual. If the Mosaic Covenant had been everlasting, it would have been unnecessary to state that its various features were likewise everlasting. The Sabbath, therefore, was distinguished as perpetual because the Mosaic was not. Nevertheless, the NT gives us great liberty in fulfilling its requirement.

The next covenant also was given within the context of the Mosaic. This was the promise to Phinehas of a "covenant of an everlasting priesthood" (*Numbers 25:13*). This covenant, as with the Sabbath, stood in contrast to the Mosaic covenant. If the Mosaic had been everlasting, it would have been redundant to offer Phinehas, the Levite, an everlasting priesthood, since all the specifications of the Mosaic already would have been understood as everlasting, including the provision of an everlasting priesthood for the Levites. This covenant with Phinehas was called "everlasting" also because its promise was a done deal, and ultimately would be fulfilled in the priesthood of all believers (*Exodus 19:6; 1 Peter 2:5*).

The next divinely commissioned covenant concerned David. This too was an "everlasting" covenant. (*2 Samuel 23:5; Isaiah 55:3*)

The Mosaic Covenant is sharply contrasted with the others. Why is a covenant that is so important and central not regarded as everlasting? Fulfillment of the everlasting covenants depended on one thing—the faithfulness of God to keep His promises. In contrast, the Mosaic depended on the faithfulness of humankind. Scripture always radically distinguishes the two: God's faithfulness is certain, while ours is a twisted mess (*Psalm 14:1*).

THE MOSAIC COVENANT WAS INADEQUATE

The New Testament maintains that although the Mosaic Covenant wasn't flawed, it was inadequate (*Romans 8:3; 7:5; Hebrews 7:18–19; 10:1*). A hammer might be perfectly crafted, but it wasn't designed to drill a hole; likewise, the Mosaic Covenant was perfect, but it wasn't designed to defeat sin and backsliding. This is not simply a Christian rationalization; the Hebrew Scriptures support this interpretation.

The Mosaic Covenant was conditional: if Israel was obedient, she would receive blessing; if disobedient, she would be cursed (*Leviticus 26; Deuteronomy 28–29*). The Mosaic "promises" depended on the obedience of Israel to God's commands. In contrast, the Noahic covenant was unconditional: God promised He would never again destroy the world with a flood as He had done, saving only Noah and his family.

The conditional nature of the Mosaic Covenant meant that when Israel sinned and required God's mercy, she could not appeal to the promises of the covenant. These would bring only condemnation. Israel, instead, had to appeal to former promises from the "covenant of your fathers" (*Deuteronomy 4:30–31; see also Leviticus 26:42–45*).

THE MOSAIC COVENANT WAS GRACE-DEFICIENT

Israel's hope had to come from the patriarchal (Abrahamic) or Davidic Covenant. We find no Hebrew prophet crying out, "God will remember the covenant that He made with Moses and have mercy on you!" Almost all of the prophets explicitly proclaim the restoration of Israel, but not as a result of Israel's obedience to the Law. The Law, instead, had brought condemnation. Its requirement that the curses had to be brought on Israel (*Deuteronomy 27:26*) would have to be set aside in order for Israel to find mercy.

The Law was inadequate, because it could never provide what Israel needed. Israel's problems were much deeper. Israel needed more than rules upheld by positive and negative reinforcements; she needed a change of heart—the very thing she lacked. Moses had promised "stiff-necked" Israel that, sometime in the future, God would "circumcise your heart and the heart of your descendants, to love the Lord your God with all your heart and with all your soul, that you may live" (*Deuteronomy 30:6*). Israel needed a circumcised heart in order to love God and live, but that hadn't happened yet. It was like telling Israel that she was doomed to failure!

More to the point, Moses told Israel, "Yet the Lord has not given you a heart to perceive and eyes to see and ears to hear, to this very day" (*Deuteronomy 29:4*). Something had to change. Israel lacked a heart for God despite all of her proclamations otherwise. She would turn her heart from the covenant, and tragedy would overtake her. Moses was prophetically explicit about this in a song that God directed him to teach Israel about a man who symbolized Israel: "Then he forsook God who made him" (*Deuteronomy 32:15*).

This is exactly what Israel would do despite all the Mosaic warnings. Moses was sure of it: "For I know that after my death you will become utterly corrupt, and turn aside from the way which I have commanded you. And evil will befall you in the latter days, because you will do evil in the sight of the Lord, to provoke Him to anger through the work of your hands" (*Deuteronomy 31:29*).

Joshua reiterated this message of gloom to Israel in the midst of Israel's protestations to the contrary (*Joshua 24:19*). The Mosaic covenant couldn't be everlasting. It would have been an everlasting failure. It had to be replaced!

Such predictions of failure are not to be found in other religious or political literature. No politician ever put forth a program and then stated unequivocally that it was doomed to fail. Hebrew Scriptures would not contain such negative messages unless they were true and unless the people were divinely convinced that they were God's very words, even though they didn't like the messages.

THE MOSAIC COVENANT HAD TO BE REPLACED

God promised Israel that she would be a nation of priests (*Exodus 19:6; Isaiah 61:6*) and that He would dwell in her midst (*Leviticus 26:11–12; Joel 3:17, 21*). Her present situation, however, directly contradicted these promises. She couldn't bear God's presence (*Exodus 20:19*), and He couldn't bear hers (*Exodus 33:2–3*). God would meet with Moses in the tent of meeting, but this tent was placed far outside the camp and no one except Moses and Joshua could approach it (*Exodus 33:7*).

The Temple also communicated the same forbidding presence of the Lord: only the priests could enter into the Holy Place, and only the high priest could enter into the High Holy Place, and only once a year. When they did enter, it could only be after they had fulfilled every requirement (*Leviticus 16:2*). God's presence was a terrifying reality. This was quite different from what Israel had been promised. Israel was supposed to be so intimate with God that their relationship was described as a marriage (*Hosea 2:18-19; Isaiah 62:4*). In order for this portrait to be realized, the Law and its Temple curtain of separation would have to come down.

The institution of the Temple offerings also conveyed the inadequacy of the Mosaic Law and covenant. The fact that they had to be offered continually meant that these offerings did not cover subsequent sins; thus, whenever an Israelite entertained a covetous thought, he was again in sin and therefore deserved to be cursed. The sacrifices also failed to remove the discomforting thoughts of this terrifying God; Israel was promised curses for every infraction (*Deuteronomy 27:15–26*).

It is perhaps most significant that the Mosaic covenant never offered the promise of eternal life. If Law-keeping couldn't guarantee eternal life, what good was it?

It wasn't that the concept of eternal life was entirely absent from the Mosaic revelation. Jesus used *Exodus 3:6* to correct the Sadducees who denied the resurrection: "I am the God of your father—the God of Abraham, the God of Isaac, and the God of Jacob" (emphasis added). This proved that the three patriarchs were still living, since God didn't say that He *was* their God, but that He *is* their God. The Law, instead, was disturbingly non-explicit regarding how to obtain this eternal life. This was evidently another way that God hinted to Israel that the Mosaic covenant was temporary and would be superseded by a new covenant that guaranteed eternal life.

THE MOSAIC COVENANT IS NOT PART OF THE ULTIMATE SOLUTION

The portrait that emerges from Hebrew Scriptures does not show Israel as finally developing more self-control and obedience to perform the Mosaic Law successfully in order to secure blessing and deliverance. According to prophecy, God's eventual deliverance will not come because Israel wakes up, smells the coffee, and repents on her own. God will have to initiate Israel's return. "For the Lord will judge His people and have compassion on His servants, when He sees that their power is gone" (*Deuteronomy 32:36*).

It is not any positive act of Israel's that will warrant God's deliverance; rather, it is Israel's destitution that will move God. According to Moses, Israel will violate the Mosaic Covenant and bring down on herself the promised curses. It is God who then will have "compassion." According to Jeremiah, this will be through a "new covenant" (*Jeremiah 31:31–34*), implemented in a radically different way. Moses knew that Israel would fail and that her problem was one of the heart, and if Israel had a heart problem, she would need a heart answer (*Deuteronomy 30:6*).

Israel, without a changed heart, inevitably went astray. She needed to be born again with a new heart. She needed a covenant that would go much further than the Mosaic.

THE NEW COVENANT SUPERSEDES THE OLD

Ezekiel states that even though Israel consistently disgraced God before the other nations, God would act lovingly on her behalf. Ezekiel writes, "I will cleanse you from all your filthiness and from all your idols. I will give you a new heart and put a new spirit within you; I will take the heart of stone out of your flesh and give you a heart of flesh. I will put My Spirit within you" (*Ezekiel 36:25-27; see also 11:19-20*).

174

The very thing Israel had lacked under the Old, she would receive under the New—a new heart and the indwelling Holy Spirit. Jeremiah associates this necessary change with a new and permanent covenant: "Then I will give them one heart and one way that they may fear Me forever, for the good of them and their children after them. And I will make an EVERLASTING covenant with them, that I will not turn away from doing them good; but I will put My fear in their hearts so that they will NOT DEPART from Me" (*Jeremiah 32:39-40*).

There is the guarantee of a hope here that isn't found under the Mosaic covenant. As a result of God's New Covenant grace, "they will not depart from me." This is why the Mosaic Covenant couldn't be called "eternal." As long as blessing depended on Israel, no guarantee could be made; but if it depended on God, He could make an ironclad guarantee. How could God guarantee that He would always bless Israel if His blessings depended on Israel's obedience? He would change Israel's heart to ensure her obedience.

In contrast to the Mosaic Covenant, which was followed by cycles of rebellion and devastation for the people of Israel, the New Covenant would be characterized by unending peace. "Moreover I will make a covenant of peace with them, and it shall be an everlasting covenant with them; I will establish them and multiply them, and I will set My sanctuary in their midst forevermore. My tabernacle also shall be with them; indeed I will be their God, and they shall be My people" (*Ezekiel 37:26-27; see also 34:25-26; Isaiah 54:9-10*).

The terms "sanctuary" and "tabernacle" in this context shouldn't be taken literally as actual buildings, which would call to mind the Mosaic covenant, but figuratively (e.g., *Amos 9:11; 2 Samuel 7:11; Zechariah 6:12-13*). The intimacy between God and His people makes a building unnecessary and counterproductive. He will be the sanctuary. Walls will no longer separate. God will enter into the most intimate form of relationship with His people. Hosea points to a future, radical covenant that would ensure God's unfailing love: "In that day I [God] will make a covenant..../ I will betroth you to Me forever;/ Yes, I will betroth you to Me / In righteousness and justice, / In lovingkindness and mercy" (*Hosea 2:18-19*; *Isaiah 62:4*).

This wasn't a covenant that already had been in place. God says, "I will make a covenant!" It would be a "forever" covenant. Significantly, God lays down no conditions that Israel must fulfill in order to enter into her blessedness, as had been characteristic of the Mosaic Covenant. God, instead, will enter into a permanent relationship with Israel; He will marry His people. Hosea had been instructed to take his adulterous wife Gomer into seclusion; likewise, God would unilaterally do the same for Israel through His gift of faith.

The idea of a marriage with God must have seemed somewhat blasphemous to Mosaic Israel. Her experience had been characterized by God's words to Moses: "Tell Aaron your brother not to come at just any time into the Holy Place inside the veil, before the mercy seat which is on the ark, lest he die" (*Leviticus16:2*). This was quite different from the intimacy of marriage. The features of the Mosaic Covenant did not allow for such a reality. This temporary covenant would have to be replaced.

Isaiah concurs that this "yet to be" covenant would be everlasting: "For I, the Lord...will make with them an everlasting covenant. / Their descendants shall be known among the Gentiles, / And their offspring among the people. / All who see them shall acknowledge them, / That they are the posterity whom the Lord has blessed" (*Isaiah 61:8-9*). Under the old covenant, God's people were to be separated from the contaminating influence of other peoples. Under the New Covenant, God's people would be among the nations.

Could the Mosaic have merely been emended to accommodate these radical changes? No. A covenant is a contract to which no one could add or subtract (*Deuteronomy 4:2*). Changes would require a New Covenant and fresh blood to seal it. The Mosaic, therefore, would "no longer be remembered" (*Jeremiah 3:14-16*).

Many verses state that God will have mercy on His people, but none of them affirm that God will have mercy by virtue of the covenant He made with Moses. His mercy, instead, is based on something radically different. The prophetic passages that we have examined look beyond a redemption based on offerings mediated by the Levitical priesthood to a redemption based on God's unmediated intervention.

A NEW ATONEMENT

Deuteronomy 32 contains the song that Moses taught Israel. It represents both a disturbing warning and a prophetic overview of Israel's blessing, rebellion, and eventual deliverance. The song surprisingly ends on a positive note:

- Rejoice, O nations, with his people, for he will avenge the blood of his servants; he will take vengeance on his enemies and make atonement for his land and people. (*Deuteronomy 32:43*)

If the Mosaic system had been adequate, this task of "atonement" would not have fallen on God but rather on the Levites, who had been divinely commissioned to provide atonement. The Levites and the Mosaic system are prophetically absent, however, at the time of Israel's eventual deliverance. Scripture never portrays them as part of the answer. (The Mosaic system, however, does play an important role as the schoolmaster that reveals our desperate need for a Savior (*Romans 3:19 20; Galatians 3:22 24*). It is

177

never the Mosaic system that comes to the rescue, but God Himself:

- Help us, O God our Savior, for the glory of your name; deliver us and forgive our sins for your name's sake. (*Psalm 79:9; also 65:3*)

A new High Priest, in line with the priesthood of the enigmatic Melchizedek (*Psalm 110:4*), would trump the Levitical priesthood, which required that all priests had to come from the tribe of Levi, according to the Mosaic covenant. This "King of Righteousness" took the scriptural stage only once—three verses worth (*Genesis 14:18-20*)—but he made an enduring impact, partly because he was both a king and a priest, something forbidden under Mosaic Law. This suggests a change.

Likewise, Zechariah prophesied about a distant individual who would also be a "priest on His throne." This person would "build the temple of the Lord" (*Zechariah 6:13*). Christianity understands that Jesus "built" this very temple through His incarnation, taking on the form of a man and "tabernacling" among us (*John 1:14; 2:19*).

Along with a radically different High Priest, Scripture prophesies a new priesthood. God promised Israel that she would be a nation of priests (*Exodus 19:6; Isaiah 61:6*), something she had never experienced. This nation of priests would necessarily replace the Levitical order that restricted priesthood to Levites.

At first glance, this seems to contradict the New Testament promise that all believers would be priests (*1 Peter 2:5, 9; Revelation1:6*). How could Israel assume the promised priesthood when this was a standing promise to all believers? This is easily reconciled by recognizing that Israel also must come to a faith in Christ in order to receive her promised priesthood along with *all* other believers.

This understanding also helps us reconcile the more difficult verses. Jeremiah said that to the degree that God's promises to David are unshakable, they are equally unshakable to the Levites (*Jeremiah 33:18, 20-21; Numbers 25:12-13*). On the surface, this is troubling for Christianity: if the Levitical priesthood remains, so must the Mosaic Covenant, right? The prophecies, however, do not say that the Levitical priesthood will remain unchanged. They merely state that God will remain faithful to the Levitical priests. They will become priests according to the same promise that will make all Israel priests. There are other ways to function as priests besides offering animal sacrifices. God instructed Israel to offer the "sacrifice (literally "calves") of our lips" as her offering of repentance (*Hosea 14:2; see also Psalm 69:30-31; 50:13-14*), not actual calves.

Levitical atonement was sorely inadequate. God had to pay the price of atonement. His atonement would provide the basis of the everlasting covenant:

- And I will establish My covenant with you. Then you shall know that I am the Lord, that you may remember and be ashamed, and never open your mouth anymore because of your shame, when I provide you an atonement for all you have done (*Ezekiel 16:62-63*).

This covenant was not to be based on any Levitical functions, but on the unilateral grace of God as promised in the covenant God made with Abraham (*Deuteronomy 32:43; Psalm 79:9; 19:14; Isaiah 35:9-10; Zechariah 3:8-9*).

Israel's hope had always been Messianic, not Mosaic. It looked toward a Redeemer who would refine Israel with His "fire" (*Malachi 3:2*), rather than the sprinkling of animal blood, which God never ultimately desired (*Psalm 51:16-17*):

- Behold, I send My messenger, and he will prepare the way before Me. And the Lord, whom you seek, will suddenly come to His temple, even the Messenger of the covenant, in whom you delight. Behold, He is coming," says the Lord of hosts. "But who can endure the day of His coming? And who can stand when He appears? For He is like a refiner's fire and like launderers' soap. (*Malachi 3:1–2*).

The "Messenger of the covenant" is no less than God Himself, coming to make His atonement. He is "the Lord," and it is "His" temple. He is the "refiner's fire," something that can only pertain to God. He will purify His people.

A NEW BLOOD OFFERING

A New Covenant requires a new blood offering (Exodus 24:8; *Hebrews 9:18*). An everlasting covenant requires a special blood offering:

- This is what the LORD says: "In the time of my favor I will answer you, and in the day of salvation I will help you; I will keep you and will make you to be a covenant for the people (*Isaiah 49:8; see also 42:6*).

To whom does "You" refer? Virtually all Christian and some Jewish exegetes agree that the Messiah Himself is the covenant. It is His death that will seal the covenant, and His life that is the substance of the covenant. It is His blood that will release us from sin and death. Zechariah adds:

- Rejoice greatly, O daughter of Zion! Shout, O daughter of Jerusalem! Behold, your King is coming to you; He is just and having salvation, lowly and riding on a donkey, a colt, the foal of a donkey….He shall speak peace to the nations; His dominion shall be from 'sea to sea, and from the River to the ends of the earth.' As for you also, because of the blood of your covenant, I will set your prisoners free from the waterless pit (*Zechariah 9:9–11*).

The King who comes "riding on a donkey" is the Messiah, of course (*Matthew 21:5*), and the covenant that will secure freedom for "your prisoners" is the New Covenant (*Isaiah 61:1, 8*). The "blood of your covenant," therefore, must be more potent than the blood of animals, which failed to secure true, even temporary forgiveness (*Romans 3:25*). This new blood will seal a covenant of monumental proportions. The Levites play no role here.

It's clear that Israel's hope wasn't in the Mosaic system but in a Savior who Himself would provide atonement. That's why He is often called the "Redeemer" (e.g., *Job 19:25; Psalm 19:14; 78:35; Isaiah 41:14; 43:14; 44:6, 24; 47:4*). It is the Redeemer who ultimately will provide the payment to deliver His people from sin (*Psalm 49:15*). That's why His people are called the "ransomed" or the "redeemed" (Isaiah 35:9-10; 51:11; 62:12). Redemption is never accomplished on the basis of Israel's righteousness, but on the Lord's (*Psalm 85:13*).

How does the Mosaic Covenant fit into this portrait of grace? It is "holy and righteous" (*Romans 7:12; Psalm 119*), but it is never portrayed as the source of hope; it is, rather, the source of condemnation that points to the Hope:

- Is the law then against the promises of God? Certainly not! For if there had been a law given which could have given life, truly righteousness would have been by the law. But the Scripture has confined all under sin that the promise by faith in Jesus Christ might be given to those who believe. But before faith came, we were kept

181

under guard by the law, kept for the faith which would afterward be revealed. Therefore the law was our tutor to bring us to Christ, that we might be justified by faith. (*Galatians 3:21-24*)

The New Testament's understanding of the Old is more accurate than the understanding of the rabbis. How could it be possible that the unsophisticated writers of the New get it right, while the rabbinic scholars of the Old miss it? We can only conclude that the writers of the New had been divinely inspired.

The Old and the New are elegantly, even divinely, woven together. They are part of one cloth, the one plan of God. This points to the fact that the Bible had One Author, God Himself. (*2 Peter 1:20-21*)

The deep and profound consistency of the entire Bible demonstrates the fact that it is "God-breathed" in its entirety (*2 Timothy 3:16*). Seeing this has proven a tremendous encouragement to my faith.

WORKS CITED

1. All Bible quotations are from the New King James Version.

2. Sigal, Gerald, *The Jew and the Christian Missionary: A Jewish Response to Missionary Christianity* (New York: KTAV Publishing House, 1981)

Chapter 17

IS THE SHEDDING OF BLOOD NECESSARY FOR FORGIVENESS?

One of the best ways to demonstrate the New and Old Testament unity is to compare the understanding of the rabbis with that of the NT (WRITERS). We find that the rabbinic sages of Israel miss the meaning of their Hebrew Scriptures, while the writers of the NT are spot-on. This suggests that these uneducated men had been inspired from above.

According to the New Testament, forgiveness requires the sacrifice of a substitute: "The law requires that nearly everything be cleansed with blood, and without the shedding of blood there is no forgiveness" (*Hebrews 9:22*, NIV). However, since the destruction of the temple in AD 70, Orthodox Judaism has tended to regard the Old Testament sacrifices as unnecessary. In favor of this point of view, Rabbi David Rosen writes, "Judaism does not accept the idea of vicarious [substitutionary] atonement. We can only atone for our own sins and are responsible for our own actions." (Kendall/Rosen, 109-110)

If animal sacrifice is necessary (and the temple no longer exists) then the Christian claim that Messiah has fulfilled and replaced them becomes compelling. This represents a threat to Judaism. If, however, animal sacrifice wasn't necessary, why then had God commanded it? For its symbolic value! Rosen writes:

- Our ancient sages affirm that…"sincere repentance and works of lovingkindness (charity) are the real intercessors before God's throne" (*TB Shabbat 32A*) and that "sincere repentance is the equivalent to the rebuilding of the Temple, the restoration of the altar and

183

the offering of all the sacrifices" (*TB Sanhedrin 43B*). In terms of Jewish understanding of the sacrificial rites in the temple, while the blood of the sacrifice did indeed represent life, it was seen precisely in a representational role symbolizing "the complete yielding up of the worshipper's life to God" (*Hertz, Pentateuch and Haftorahs*). (Kendall/Rosen, 109)

While the New Testament understands the sacrificial system as a foreshadowing of the once-and-for-all substitutionary offering of God's Son, much of Rabbinic Judaism maintains that it represents the yielded life. (However, this latter view is hard to maintain in light of Mosaic revelation. Unblemished animals, representing sinlessness, were substituted for Israel's sins. That's why the Israelite had to place his hands on the sacrificial offering (*Leviticus 1:4; 4:4, 15, 29, 33*), confessing and conferring his sins on it (*Leviticus 16:21*). The Orthodox Jewish columnist, David Klinghoffer, also argues in favor of divine forgiveness without blood: "The idea that penitence was not enough would have come as a surprise to the large majority of first-century Jews, who lived in the Diaspora and therefore had no regular access to the Temple rites. In not availing themselves of these rites at all times, they were relying on scripture, which taught that forgiveness could be secured without sacrifice" (Klinghoffer, 111). Klinghoffer supports this claim by citing Solomon's prayer at the consecration of the temple as proof:

- And when they return to You with all their heart and with all their soul in the land of their enemies who led them away captive, and pray to You toward their land which You gave to their fathers, the city which You have chosen and the temple which I have built for Your name: then hear in heaven Your dwelling place their prayer and their supplication, and maintain their cause, and forgive Your people who have sinned against You, and all their transgressions which they have transgressed against You; and grant them compassion before those who took them captive, that they may have compassion on them (*1 King 8:48–50*).

For Klinghoffer, this constitutes proof that a sacrificial offering isn't necessary. This is odd. How could Solomon, on the one hand, bless the inauguration of his costly, God-ordained temple, while, at the same time, preach that the temple wasn't necessary? There are, instead, other ways to explain the fact that God would forgive the Israelites without an immediate temple sacrifice. Simply because blood wasn't required at that time doesn't mean it wasn't required! A bank will grant a loan, without a present outlay of money, if repayment is guaranteed. The loan doesn't represent a free ride, but a postponement of payment. Similarly, God could postpone payment of the debt in view of the Messianic guarantor (*Genesis 15:8–21; Hebrews 9:26*), even for the sins that had formerly been committed during the first covenant (*Hebrews 9:15*). (This same reasoning can also reconcile other verses that seem to suggest that a covering ("kipper") could be obtained by means other than blood. In any event, these verses can't be used to overturn the many explicit verses requiring blood sacrifice.)

Even though the sacrificial system was symbolic, the shedding of blood was also a requirement (*Leviticus 16:34*) through which God passed over Israel's sins (*Romans 3:25*). Thus, it couldn't simply be set aside or lose its potency, but had to be fulfilled by a once-and-for-all bloody atonement (*Hebrews 10:14*), through which God Himself would make atonement (*Deuteronomy 32:43*).

AN UNNECESSARY SYSTEM IS A WASTEFUL SYSTEM

The expenditures underlying the temple system were tremendous. Add to this the cost of maintaining the priesthood and the lives of multitudes of animals. It seems unreasonable that God would require this merely as a symbol that Israel should live in submission to God.

SACRIFICES WERE A REQUIREMENT

The sacrificial system had been so central to God's workings with Israel that Moses and Aaron informed Pharaoh, "The God of the Hebrews has met with us. Please, let us go three days' journey into the desert and sacrifice to the Lord our God, lest He fall upon us with pestilence or with the sword" (*Exodus 5:3*).

Either Israel would sacrifice animals or they would be sacrificed. Christian apologist Michael Brown correctly concludes, "The very reason God gave for calling his people out of Egypt was to offer sacrifices to him" (Brown, Michael, 73). He adds, "A careful study of the Five Books of Moses indicates that more chapters are devoted to the subject of sacrifices and offerings than to the subjects of Sabbath observance, high holy days, idolatry, adultery, murder, and theft combined" (Brown, 73). Indeed, Moses explicitly states that the blood offering was necessary to cover or atone for sins (*Leviticus 17:11*). Sacrifice was never optional. When the Angel of Death destroyed the firstborn from the land of Egypt, he passed over and spared those Israelite homes that had the blood of the offering on them (*Exodus 12:23*). Any firstborn without the blood on his doorposts would have been killed. Blood was also required to cover all the sins of Israel (*Leviticus 16:21–22*) in accordance with the New Testament (*Hebrews 9:22*).

Anti-Missionary Rabbi Tovia Singer also asserts that animal sacrifice was unnecessary: "The prophets loudly declared to the Jewish people that the contrite prayer of the penitent sinner replaces the sacrificial system" (Singer, www.outreachjudaism.org). He assumes that since Israel no longer had its temple, prayer and repentance would now suffice. He cites *Hosea 14:2–3* to prove that the sacrificial system had been replaced by "words": "Take words with you, and return to the Lord. Say to Him, 'Take away all iniquity; Receive us graciously, for we will offer the sacrifices ['bulls' in Hebrew] of our lips.'"

Singer is correct in pointing out that Hosea foresees "words" replacing the offering of "bulls." This change, however, is associated only with the culmination of the old system, starting with the Cross, as illustrated by God's declaration that "I will heal their backsliding, I will love them freely, for My anger has turned away from him" (*Hosea 14:4*). (This conclusion follows from *Hosea 14:4* because God's healing of Israel's backsliding is only accomplished at the end (*Jeremiah 32: 37-41; Ezekiel 36:25-27*). Therefore, it wasn't a matter of blood sacrifices being unnecessary, but rather being fulfilled!

SACRIFICES COULD NOT BE SET ASIDE UNDER MOSES' LAW

There is nothing in the Mosaic covenant that suggests that sacrifices were an option or that they would be abrogated apart from the Messianic atonement of Jesus. (Although the poor could offer grain as a sin offering, this was only because this offering was laid alongside a blood offering (*Leviticus 5:12*). Even so, there are a number of verses that communicate God's displeasure with the offerings (*Psalm 50:8–15; Proverbs 15:8; 21:3; Isaiah 1:11–17; Jeremiah 7:23; Amos 5:21–27; Hosea 6:6*). Such passages, however, in no way indicate that God was doing away with offerings and leaving no substitutionary blood offering in their place. Instead, these verses can be explained in either of two other ways:

First, God's displeasure didn't reflect a problem with the offerings themselves, but the hypocrisy of the offerers. *Psalm 51:16–19* illustrates this:

- For You do not desire sacrifice, or else I would give it; You do not delight in burnt offering. The sacrifices of God are a broken spirit, a broken and a contrite heart— these, O God, You will not despise.…Then You shall be pleased with the sacrifices of righteousness, with burnt offering and whole burnt offering; then they shall offer bulls on Your altar.

God was "pleased…with burnt offerings" when they were offered with a broken and repentant heart. When they were offered hypocritically, however, God refused to hear the prayers of Israel (*Isaiah 1:15*). In this regard, the esteemed Jewish thinker, Abraham Joshua Heschel wrote, "Of course, the prophets did not condemn the practice of sacrifice in itself; otherwise we should have to conclude that Isaiah intended to discourage the practice of prayer.…Men may not drown out the cries of the oppressed with the noise of hymns, nor buy off the Lord with increased offerings. The prophets disparaged the cult [of animal sacrifice] when it became a substitute for righteousness. (Brown, 86)

Second, the other verses that assert that God didn't desire the blood of animals (even though He commanded it) are explained by understanding that animal blood was merely a symbol of the ultimate Messianic offering. Israel had a dim understanding that something had to take the place of the Mosaic system and that the repeated offering of the same sacrifices gave Israel only a temporary reprieve (*Hebrews 10:1–4*). They also had been graphically instructed by the temple and offerings that intimacy with God was not yet a reality. They could not enter into God's presence (nor did they dare to!), and yet, they had been promised betrothal to their God (*Hosea 2:18–19*). Furthermore, they had been promised a "New Covenant" through which their sins would truly and permanently be forgiven (*Jeremiah 31:31–34*). Consistent with this understanding, *Psalm 40:6–8* declares that Israel's God was preparing a sacrifice that would put an end to all other sacrifices:

- "Sacrifice and offering You did not desire, but a body You have prepared for Me. In burnt offerings and sacrifices for sin You had no pleasure. Then I said, 'Behold, I have come—in the volume of the book it is written of Me—to do Your will, O God'" (*Hebrews 10:5–7 quoting Psalm 40:6–8*). (*Hebrews* quotes the Septuagint, the Greek translation of the Old Testament. In this instance, the text differs from its competitor, the Masoretic text. Although the Masoretic doesn't read, "A body you have prepared for me," both texts read, "Behold, I have come to do thy will!" This "coming" seems to suggest a replacement of the sacrificial system.)

After the two times where *Psalm 40* dismisses animal sacrifice, it then presents a human body, suggesting that the latter sacrifice will take the place of the former. This shouldn't have been foreign to Israelite ears. They often had been promised, starting with Moses (*Deuteronomy 32:43*), that God Himself would atone in the end for Israel's sins.

NEVER A MATTER OF EITHER BLOOD OR REPENTANCE

Although Job had never been short on animal sacrifices, Elihu counseled him that a special ransom was required in addition to repentance (*Job 33:24–28*). (It might be objected that citing Elihu is not persuasive. However, in context Elihu's words are just as authoritative as those that follow. Notice how his words blend thematically, without break or interruption by *Job*, into God's beginning in *38:1*.) Tovia Singer claims, however, that there are three types of atonement (sacrificial, repentance, alms), and that any one will suffice! This is contradicted, however, by the fact that any one of them by itself was incapable of bringing forgiveness:

189

- Speak to the children of Israel: 'When a man or woman commits any sin that men commit in unfaithfulness against the Lord, and that person is guilty, then he shall [1] confess the sin which he has committed. He shall [2] make restitution for his trespass in full…in addition to the [3] ram of the atonement with which atonement is made for him' (*Numbers 5:6–8, see also Leviticus 5:5–6*).

Similarly, Gerald Sigal writes, "It is clear from the Scriptures that sin is removed through genuine remorse and sincere repentance." In support, he cites *Micah 6:8*, stating that the Lord requires justice and mercy (Sigal, 16). However, this also falls short of proving that sacrifice isn't part of the equation.

Blood atonement, without confession and repentance, never accomplished anything (*Amos 5:21–24*). Nevertheless, it was still mandatory. There is no biblical evidence that it was or could be simply set aside apart from the Messiah's coming. After surveying the rabbinic literature, Michael Brown concludes, "It was only after the Temple was destroyed [in AD 70] that the Talmudic rabbis came up with the concept that God had provided other forms of atonement aside from blood. (Brown, 111)

PROPHECY: A RANSOM AND REDEEMER

There had to be the payment of a ransom. Even in the midst of God's earliest response to humankind's sin, a ransom was cryptically provided when He replaced the first couple's inadequate fig leaves with animal skins (*Genesis 3:21*), foreshadowing His Messianic endgame (*Isaiah 61:10*). A ransom is inseparably and necessarily connected to Israel's return to God (*Isaiah 35:10; 48:20; 51:10–11*). "'He who scattered Israel will gather him, and keep him as a shepherd does his flock.' For the Lord has redeemed Jacob, and ransomed him from the hand of one stronger than he" (*Jeremiah 31:10–11*).

God himself would have to pay the ransom. The Israelite couldn't afford it (*Psalm 49:7–9*)! So God Himself would pay the price (*49:15*): "I have blotted out, like a thick cloud, your transgressions, and like a cloud, your sins. Return to Me, for I have redeemed you" (*Isaiah 44:22*).

Without God's ransom, Israel couldn't return to God (*Psalm 65:3–5; 78:38; 130:7–8; Deuteronomy 32:43; Isaiah 54:5–8; Hosea 13:12–14*). Although repentance is necessary, it isn't sufficient (*Isaiah 59:16–20*). *Psalm 24* offers a graphic, if perhaps cryptic, demonstration of this principle. It asks the question, "Who may stand in His holy place!" The answer is discouraging—only those who are perfect (*Psalm 15*)! Because of this dismal response, even the gates are hanging their heads in despair, until the mysterious appearance of the "King of Glory" entering through the temple gate into God's presence to make intercession!

MESSIAH WOULD PAY WITH HIS OWN BLOOD.

Singer asserts, "Nor does Scripture ever tell us that an innocent man can die as an atonement for the sins of the wicked" (Singer, p#?). However, according to the Zohar, the most highly esteemed Jewish mystical book, in its commentary on *Isaiah 53:5*, "The children of the world are members of one another, and when the Holy One desires to give healing to the world, He smites one just man amongst them, and for his sake heals all the rest" (Brown, 157). Israel's salvation depended on Messiah's substitutionary atoning death and not on the Israelites sufficiently yielding themselves: "Break forth into joy, sing together…For the Lord has comforted His people, He has redeemed Jerusalem. The Lord has made bare His holy arm" (*Isaiah 52:9–10; cf. 59:16; 63:5*). His "holy arm," the Son (*53:1*), will pay the price: "But he was pierced for our transgressions, he was crushed for our iniquities; the punishment that brought us peace was upon him, and by his wounds we are healed. We all, like sheep, have gone astray, each of us has turned to his own way; and the LORD has laid on him the iniquity of us all (*Isaiah 53:5–7*, emphases added; see also *Psalm 40:6–8; Daniel 9:24–27; Zechariah 12:10–13:1, 7; Psalm 22; 69*).

Singer maintains that God's provision of a ram in the place of Isaac (*Genesis 22*) proved that He would never accept a human sacrifice: "When Abraham was ready to sacrifice Isaac, the Almighty admonished him that He did not want the human sacrifice…The Almighty's directive—that He only wanted animal sacrifices rather than human sacrifices—was immediately understood. This teaching has never departed from the mind and soul of the faithful children of Israel" (Singer, Pg#?)   This, however, wasn't the lesson that Israel learned, but rather the lesson was that God would provide: "And Abraham called the name of the place, The-Lord-Will-Provide; as it is said to this day, 'In the Mount of The Lord it shall be provided'" (*Genesis 22:14*). Additionally, it was more than just a matter of God's faithfulness. It was also prophetic of Messiah's atonement. The mountain wasn't named "The Lord-has-provided," but that He will provide! Nor was the promise that God would provide in general! Instead, God would provide a greater offering (overshadowing what He had already provided) "in the mount of the Lord," a phrase that "referred to the Temple mount in Jerusalem" (NIV, 38).   This became the very place that God did provide for our sins on the Cross at Calvary.

Rather than symbolizing our yielded lives, the animal sacrifices symbolized the very opposite—our unyielded, condemnation-worthy lives. That's why every Israelite had to confess his sins on the head of the sacrificial animal, which paid the price for his unyieldedness. In this way, the Israelite was taught that his hope couldn't be in his own righteousness or virtue (*Deuteronomy 27:26*), but in a perfect substitution.

Blood has a lot to say about grace. It speaks eloquently about God's ultimate ransom. After I debated Rabbi Yossi Mizrachi at Temple Gabriel, Queens, New York, an Orthodox Jew from his congregation called me. When I mentioned God's grace toward King David, he protested, "You don't understand. The Talmud explains that Bathsheba's husband Uriah was an evil man who deserved to die. Besides, Bathsheba had already been divorced from him. And so David had done righteously by killing Uriah and marrying Bathsheba!" Fortunately, David didn't see things according to the Talmud. He confessed his sins (*2 Samuel 12:13*) and acknowledged the blessedness of God's grace (*Psalm 32:1–2*) and His willingness to receive blood offerings from the sin-broken repentant heart (*Psalm 51:16–19*).

The Talmud likewise justifies the sin of all the patriarchs and therefore fails to recognize our profound need for grace. No wonder blood atonement can also be put away with such ease.

Oddly, the NT commentary fits the Hebrew Scriptures far more closely than that of the rabbis. What makes this possible? The inspiration that comes from above!

WORKS CITED

All Scripture quotations are from the New King James Version except where otherwise noted.

Brown, Michael, *Answering Jewish Objections to Jesus, Vol. 2* (Grand Rapids: Baker Books, 2007).   This book contains a very extensive rebuttal of rabbinic arguments.

Kendall, R.T and Rosen, David, *The Christian and the Pharisee* (New York: Faith Words, 2006)

Klinghoffer, David, *Why the Jews Rejected Jesus,* (New York: Doubleday, First Edition, 2005)

Singer,Tovia,"Cou*ld Jesus' Death Alone for Any Kind of Sin?".* https://outreachjudaism.org/

Sigal, Gerald, *The Jew and the Christian Missionary,* (New York: KTAV Publishing House, 1981)

 NIV Study Bible (Grand Rapids: Zondervan, 1985).

Chapter 18

CHRIST IN THE TORAH

Messianic prophecies can be very compelling for those who are truly seeking. Swiss-French theologian, Rene Pache (1904-1979), had argued that they are so compelling that those who reject them are without excuse (*Romans 1:20*):

- It is impossible for every sincere soul not to see there an extraordinary proof of the divine inspiration of the Holy Scripture. (Pache, 24)

To illustrate his point, Pache provided a small list of those prophecies that Jesus had literally fulfilled:

- Jesus was born of a virgin (*Isaiah 7:14; Matthew 1:22, 23*)
- In a family of David. (*Isaiah 11:1; Luke 1:32*)
- At Bethlehem. (*Micah 5:1; Matthew 2:4-6*)
- On this occasion, little children were massacred. (*Jeremiah 31:15; Matthew 2:16-18*)
- The Child Jesus was carried away into Egypt, from which He was brought back later. (*Hosea 11:1; Matthew 2:15*)
- He grew up in Galilee. (*Isaiah 8:23; 9:1; Matthew 2:22, 23*)
- He was anointed of the Spirit. (*Isaiah 11:2; Luke 4:17-21*)
- He took upon Him our maladies and our infirmities. (*Isaiah 53:3; Matthew 8:16, 17*)
- He made His entry into Jerusalem seated on an ass. (*Zechariah 9:9; Matthew 21:4, 5*)

- He was betrayed by one of His intimate friends. (*Psalm 41:10; John 13:18*)
- His disciples abandoned Him. (*Zechariah 13:7; Matthew 26:31*)
- He was sold for 30 pieces of silver which served to buy the Potter's field. (*Zechariah 11:12, 13; Matthew 26:15; 27:7, 10*)
- He was delivered to spitting and buffeting. (*Isaiah 50:6; Matthew 27:30*)
- He was offered gall and vinegar to drink. (*Psalm 69: 22; Matthew 27:34, 48*)
- Not one of His bones were broken. (*Exodus 12:46; John 19: 33, 36*)
- His feet and hands were pierced. (*Psalm 22:17; John 20:25*)
- His garments were divided and drawn by lot. (*Psalm 22:19; John 19:23, 24*)
- He was put to death among malefactors, and He had His tomb with the rich men. (*Isaiah 53:9; Matthew 27:38, 57-60*)

Even with this impressive list, there were many prophecies that Pache didn't list for one reason or another. Here are just a few from the *Book of Genesis*:

- He is the promised seed of the woman who would destroy the source of evil (*Genesis 3:15*).
- He is the seed of Abraham through whom the whole world would be blessed (*Genesis 12:1-3*).
- He would come from the tribe of David (*Genesis 49:50*).

However impressive these *explicit* messianic prophecies might be, I find myself more drawn to the *implicit* ones. Actually, there are cryptic portraits of the Messiah contained in such accounts as Jacob wrestling with the Angel, who turns out to be God (*Genesis 32*), or the mysterious portrait of God being struck down by Moses because of the sins of Israel. (*Exodus 17*)

With either type of prophecy you might prefer, both illustrate the fact that the Bible is about the Messiah. In the Old Testament, Israel looked forward to His coming; in the New, we look in both directions – back to what He has done for us and ahead to His return.

✳✳✳

One Christian challenged me with this statement: "Jesus is supposed to be found throughout the Scriptures (*John 5:39*), but I could only find one prophecy (*Deuteronomy 18:15-18*) about Him in the Torah [the Five Books of Moses]. Also, Jesus had claimed that Abraham had seen His day and was glad (*John 8:56*), but I just don't see any evidence of this in the Patriarchal accounts."

The Apostle Paul had made virtually the same claim about Abraham hearing the Gospel:

- And the Scripture, foreseeing that God would justify the Gentiles by faith, preached the gospel beforehand to Abraham, saying, "In you shall all the nations be blessed." (*Galatians 3:8*; ESV)

The *Book of Hebrews* also suggests that Abraham (along with the other Patriarchs) knew something about the Good News:

- These all died in faith, not having received the things promised, but having seen them and greeted them from afar, and having acknowledged that they were strangers and exiles on the earth. For people who speak thus make it clear that they are seeking a homeland…they desire a better country, that is, a heavenly one. Therefore God is not ashamed to be called their God, for he has prepared for them a city. (*Hebrews 11:13-14,16*)

Do we find evidence for this in the Torah, or, as the rabbis claim, do the New Testament writers see in the Torah what is not really there? If Abraham did see Jesus' day, where is the evidence from the Torah?

For one thing, Abraham had many encounters with the Divine:

- Now the LORD said to Abram, "Go from your country and your kindred and your father's house to the land that I will show you. And I will make of you a great nation, and I will bless you and make your name great, so that you will be a blessing. I will bless those who bless you, and him who dishonors you I will curse, and in you all the families of the earth shall be blessed. (*Genesis 12:1-3*)

In his earthly life, Abraham saw the fruition of only a tiny part of this prophecy. Did he have reason to believe that the rest would be fulfilled? Was he shown the Good News and the afterlife? (*Galatians 3:8*)

Afterwards, Abraham had a mysterious encounter with a priest named Melchizedek, whose name means "Righteous King." He is also variously described as the priest of the Most High God and the King of Salem—or "peace," in Hebrew. Abraham recognized His authority and gave tithes to Him (*Genesis 14:20; see also Psalm 110*). In fact, Melchizedek seems to be more than human. We are told that he had no parents:

- He is without father or mother or genealogy, having neither beginning of days nor end of life, but resembling the Son of God he continues a priest forever. (*Hebrews 7:3*)

Only God has no beginning or end. Therefore, Abraham's experience with Melchizedek must have been a Christophany – an appearance of Jesus. Why should we conclude so? We are told that no one has ever seen God, the Father (*Exodus 33:20; 1 Timothy 6:16*). Judging from Abraham's subsequent actions, this encounter seems to have been transformative for the patriarch. He gave Melchizedek a tenth of everything he had won when he rescued Lot. Why? Perhaps it was because Melchizedek had just revealed to him that his victory over the marauders had been a gift from God.

- After his return from the defeat of Chedorlaomer and the kings who were with him, the king of Sodom went out to meet him at the Valley of Shaveh (that is, the King's Valley). And Melchizedek king of Salem brought out bread and wine. (He was priest of God Most High.) And he blessed him and said, "Blessed be Abram by God Most High, Possessor of heaven and earth; and blessed be God Most High, who has delivered your enemies into your hand!" And Abram gave him a tenth of everything. (*Genesis 14:17-20*)

Right after this, the generally conniving and cowardly Abraham (*Genesis 20:13*) declared to the King of Sodom that he would take none of the plunder that had been won. Why? Evidently, Abraham must have been convinced about the *Personhood* of the Priest Melchizedek. However, this encounter also seems to fall short of the revelation of the Good News.

In the following chapter, *Genesis 15*, Abraham seems to have had another Christophany, or divine encounter with Jesus. Abraham had asked God to confirm His promises to him. God complied to the request with a covenant-making ceremony. In the forms of a blazing torch and a smoking firepot—symbols of wrath and judgment—He passed between the butchered parts of animals. In this intensely symbolic and visually striking way, God pledged to honor the promises He had made to Abraham in the Covenant.

However, dread and darkness came upon Abraham in the process, and the pledge that God had taken was associated with symbols of wrath and judgment. Why? It seems that God had been conveying to Abraham the means by which He would accomplish His promise – the judgment that He would unleash upon Himself, as Paul had explained:

- For all the promises of God find their Yes in him [Jesus]. That is why it is through him that we utter our Amen to God for his glory. (*2 Corinthians 1:20*)

Without the Cross, there would only be destruction (*Romans 6:23*). Only the Cross would allow God's glorious plan to proceed. There was no other way. Jesus had prayed for another way apart from the Cross, but He submitted to the will of the Father and to the inevitability of the Cross and His inevitable judgment upon sin.

This very theme had been reenacted in heaven for the Apostle John:

- Then I saw in the right hand of him who was seated on the throne a scroll written within and on the back, sealed with seven seals. And I saw a mighty angel proclaiming with a loud voice, "Who is worthy to open the scroll and break its seals?" And no one in heaven or on earth or under the earth was able to open the scroll or to look into it, and I began to weep loudly because no one was found worthy to open the scroll or to look into it. And one of the elders said to me, "Weep no more; behold, the Lion of the tribe of Judah, the Root of David, has conquered, so that he can open the scroll and its seven seals." (*Revelation 5:1-5*)

John's tears had been very appropriate. He understood that the redemptive plans of the Father could not proceed. However, he was failing to see the vital missing link – the Cross of Christ, which was able to pay for the sins of the world. This established the worthiness of Jesus to open the scroll.

This piece of the puzzle had been cryptically revealed at just the right time – at the time that God's "very good" creation had been torn apart by sin and rebellion. As the Son of a woman, Jesus would reverse the Fall by crushing Satan, the malevolent force behind the serpent in the Garden of Eden. However, in the process, the "serpent" would strike His heel, thinking that the victory was his. (*1 Corinthians 2:8*)

Here is what God said to the serpent after Adam and Eve had sinned:

- And I will put enmity
  between you and the woman,
  and between your offspring and hers;
  he will crush your head,
  and you will strike his heel. (*Genesis 3:15*)

Satan struck the heel of Christ on the Cross, failing to understand that his victory was actually his "death blow." This entitled God to move decisively against sin without destroying the entire world. Thus, sin was conquered through the Cross.

Why am I going into all of this detail? I am doing so to establish the case that the Gospel had been revealed to Abraham and that Christ was manifested throughout the Torah. However, I also have another purpose – to show the unity between the two Testaments, a unity which points to God's unifying authorship over the entirety of Scripture. So let's move on to the next account which is even more revealing.

Abraham had been asked to sacrifice his "only son" Isaac on Mt. Moriah (Jerusalem). (Remember that Abraham's literal firstborn was Ishmael.) This was a foreshadowing of the way that God would give "His only begotten Son" on Calvary. However, before Abraham went through with the sacrifice, the Angel of the Lord intervened and provided a ram for an offering instead of Isaac:

- And the angel of the LORD ["Yahweh"] called to Abraham a second time from heaven and said, "By myself I have sworn, declares the LORD, because you have done this and have not withheld your son, your only son, I will surely bless you…" (*Genesis 22:15-17a*)

Interestingly, Abraham understood far more about this encounter than might seem apparent. Instead of naming the mountain upon which he was to sacrifice Isaac, "God *has* provided," which would have described what had taken place, Abraham named it, "God *will* provide." This suggests that Abraham had been shown that his offering of Isaac had only been a representation of what God would one day offer on that very same mountain:

- So Abraham called the name of that place, "The LORD will provide"; as it is said to this day, "On the mount of the LORD it shall be provided." (*Genesis 22:14*)

Evidently, Israel too had understood this offering of Isaac as prophetic (EXPLAIN). And, just what would be provided? An offering similar to the one that Abraham had been asked to provide…a Father offering His Son! Perhaps Jesus was thinking of this milestone when He said:

- "Your father Abraham rejoiced that he would see my day. He saw it and was glad." (*John 8:56*)

What was it that Abraham saw? What was Jesus' "day?" It was the day of His glory:

- And Jesus answered them, "The hour has come for the Son of Man to be glorified. Truly, truly, I say to you, unless a grain of wheat falls into the earth and dies, it remains alone; but if it dies, it bears much fruit." (*John 12:23-24*)

Why did Abraham rejoice to see Jesus' day? He understood that God the Father would, on that day, offer His only-begotten Son as he (HIMSELF) had been directed to do as a foreshadowing of this Messianic event. And His offering would not only be the substitute for Abraham's son, but for the sins of the entire world.

Who was this Angel of the Lord that Abraham had encountered on Mount Moriah? In the above account, He is also called "Yahweh," a term that only refers to God. We, therefore, call these appearances "Christophanies," or "Theophanies." "The Angel of the LORD" is the phrase most closely associated with these appearances. There is evidence that this "Angel" is actually God the Son. Let's take a look at the first manifestation of this mysterious Angel when He appeared to Hagar, Abraham's concubine and the mother of Ishmael:

- The angel of the LORD found her by a spring of water in the wilderness, the spring on the way to Shur. And he said, "Hagar, servant of Sarai, where have you come from and where are you going?" She said, "I am fleeing from my mistress Sarai." The angel of the LORD said to her, "Return to your mistress and submit to her." The angel of the LORD also said to her, "I will surely multiply your offspring so that they cannot be numbered for multitude." And the angel of the LORD said to her, "Behold, you are pregnant and shall bear a son. You shall call his name Ishmael, because the LORD has listened to your affliction. He shall be a wild donkey of a man, his hand against everyone and everyone's hand against him, and he shall dwell over against all his kinsmen." So she called the name of the LORD who spoke to her, "You are a God of seeing," for she said, "Truly here I have seen him who looks after me." (*Genesis 16:7-13*)

This narrative claims that it was the LORD—Yahweh—who spoke to Hagar. Hagar claimed that she had seen God, revealed to her in the Person of the Angel of the LORD.

Two chapters later:

- The LORD [Yahweh] appeared to him [Abraham] by the oaks of Mamre, as he sat at the door of his tent in the heat of the day. (*Genesis 18:1*)

Please note that, according to *Exodus 33:20*, Yahweh—the Father—appears to no one. Therefore, this appearance must have been a Christophany of Yahweh, the Son.

Returning to the *Genesis 18* account, we see that the angels who were accompanying Yahweh began to make their way toward Sodom. But Abraham used this time as an opportunity to petition the LORD. After their conversation:

- The LORD [Yahweh, the Son] went his way, when he had finished speaking to Abraham, and Abraham returned to his place. (*Genesis 18:33*)

Many years later, Abraham's grandson Jacob wrestled all night with a "man." Jacob soon realized that this "man" was actually God:

- So Jacob called the name of the place Peniel, saying, "For I have seen God face to face, and yet my life has been delivered." (*Genesis 32:30*)

Had God revealed the Gospel to Jacob? At the end of his life, while he was blessing the sons of Joseph, Jacob identified God as the "Angel" with whom he had wrestled so many years before:

- And he [Jacob] blessed Joseph and said, "The God before whom my fathers Abraham and Isaac walked, the God who has been my shepherd all my life long to this day, the Angel who has redeemed me from all evil, bless the boys; and in them let my name be carried on, and the name of my fathers Abraham and Isaac; and let them grow into a multitude in the midst of the earth." (*Genesis 48:15-16*)

So, after Jacob had invoked "God" twice and "the Angel" a third time, he implored them (*in the* singular*)* to bless his family. Therefore, it is clear that Jacob understood that the Angel of the LORD was also God.

Here is yet another observation that confirms the identity of "the Angel of the LORD" as God: Jacob claimed that it was

205

this Angel who had "redeemed me from all evil." However, we know that it is God who is clearly identified as the Redeemer (*2 Samuel 4:9; Psalm 34:22; 121:7; Isaiah 44:22-23; 49:7*). Therefore, "the Angel of the Lord," God, and the Redeemer are all referring to the same divine Person, the second Person of the Trinity, and Jacob somehow understood that this divine Being had "redeemed" him from all of his evil. How? This Angel had allowed Himself to be physically abused while wrestling with Jacob, who ironically had been blessed in the midst of his sin (*Hosea 12:2-4*). Odd, right? Evidently, from this revealing encounter, Jacob understood that he had been redeemed. He had done evil but received the Good News of redemption and a foretaste of its blessings.

Yes – Jacob had been left crippled by this engagement, but his infirmity became his strength in the Lord (*2 Corinthians 12:7-10*). After this, we begin to observe that the life of this conniver was being changed.

Much later, the prophet Isaiah wrote that the "Angel of His Presence" had saved and redeemed Israel:

- In all their affliction He was afflicted, and the Angel of His Presence saved them; in His love and in His pity He redeemed them; and He bore them and carried them all the days of old. (*Isaiah 63:9*)

Thus, it is plain to see that Isaiah also equated this Angel with God.

Let us not overlook one of the most famous theophany, when the Angel appeared to Moses in the midst of a burning bush in the middle of the desert:

- And the angel of the LORD appeared to him in a flame of fire out of the midst of a bush. He looked, and behold, the bush was burning, yet it was not consumed. And Moses said, "I will turn aside to see this great sight, why the bush is not burned." When the LORD saw that he turned aside to see, God called to him out of the bush, "Moses, Moses!" And he said, "Here I am." (*Exodus 3:2-4*)

We should notice in these verses that this Angel is called both "LORD" and "God." All of these appearances provide us with incontrovertible evidence that God—or Yahweh—is not the single Person that the rabbis claim of God. As we have seen, the Son (manifested especially as "the Angel of the LORD") appeared on a number of occasions. Furthermore, all of these references should put to rest the rabbinic claim that God does not take on human form. Instead, these appearances of a Messianic figure provide us with powerful evidence for the Trinity.

***

The Angel of the LORD appears in many other places throughout the Pentateuch. He was the One who brought Israel out of Egypt:

- When we cried out to the Lord, He heard our voice and sent the Angel and brought us up out of Egypt... (*Numbers 20:16a*)

However, there are other verses that claim that it was the LORD who brought Israel out of Egypt:

- And the LORD went before them by day in a pillar of cloud to lead them along the way, and by night in a pillar of fire to give them light, that they might travel by day and by night. (*Exodus 13:21; see also Deuteronomy 31:2-3*)

207

There are, in addition, other verses that mention "the Angel of God." How do we resolve this apparent contradiction? From *Numbers 20:16*, it is clear that the Angel Himself is God, and yet He seems to be presented in a very distinct way, and as a very distinct Person. For, if we examine the verse again, we can see that the Lord "…heard our voice and sent the Angel…"

In the following verses, we can see once again that God differentiated Himself from His Angel:

- Behold, I send an Angel before you to keep you in the way and to bring you into the place which I have prepared. Beware of Him and obey His voice; do not provoke Him, for He will not pardon your transgressions; for My name is in Him. (*Exodus 23:20-21*)

When the Word declares that God's "name is in Him," this is the same as saying that "My essence, or nature, is in Him." This is more proof that God and the Angel are one—and yet they are distinct. In yet another verse, God the Father makes a sharp differentiation between Himself and the Divine Angel:

- And I will send My Angel before you, and I will drive out the Canaanite and the Amorite and the Hittite and the Perizzite and the Hivite and the Jebusite. Go up to a land flowing with milk and honey; for I will not go up in your midst, lest I consume you on the way, for you are a stiff-necked people. (*Exodus 33:2-3*)

From this verse, we can see that God the Father could not be in the presence of Israel. Furthermore, Scripture proclaims that the Father can never be seen because He dwells in unapproachable light:

- God, the blessed and only Ruler, the King of kings and Lord of lords, who alone is immortal and who lives in unapproachable light, whom no one has seen or can see. To him be honor and might forever. Amen. (*I Timothy 6:15b-16*)

In addition, we have these words from the Old Testament:

- But He said [to Moses], 'You cannot see My face; for no man shall see Me, and live.' (*Exodus 33:20*)

That is why God the Father sent His Angel to accompany Israel out of Egypt. Nevertheless, as it turned out, God was seen:

- So the Lord spoke to Moses face to face, as a man speaks to his friend. (*Exodus 33:11a*)

How is it that God was seen and yet cannot be seen? This dilemma is resolved when we recognize that it must have been God the Son who was seen, and not God the Father.

Let's take a look at another passage that demonstrates this truth. God had reprimanded Moses' sister and brother, who were attempting to usurp some of Moses' authority:

- And he said, 'Hear my words: If there is a prophet among you, I the LORD make myself known to him in a vision; I speak with him in a dream. Not so with my servant Moses. He is faithful in all my house. With him I speak mouth to mouth, clearly, and not in riddles, and he beholds the form of the LORD. Why then were you not afraid to speak against my servant Moses'? (*Numbers 12:6-8*)

Again, this sounds like a contradiction. Either God cannot be seen...or Moses had actually seen Him. There is an explanation that makes perfect sense: Moses had actually seen God in the person of the Angel of the LORD, the second Person of the Trinity. In an awe-inspiring Christophany on Mt. Sinai, Moses had seen a pre-incarnate manifestation of Jesus Christ.

To back up this claim, there are other proofs. Stephen, before his martyrdom, also described the giving of the Law on Mt. Sinai as an encounter with the living Christ:

- This is the one [Moses] who was in the congregation in the wilderness with the angel [of the LORD, or Christ] who spoke to him at Mount Sinai, and with our fathers...(*Acts 7:38a*)

The Apostle Paul, writing about the same scene, claimed that Moses had encountered an "intermediary":

- Why then the law? It was added because of transgressions, until the offspring should come to whom the promise had been made, and it was put in place through angels by an intermediary. (*Galatians 3:19; see also Hebrews 2:2*)

This "intermediary" was the second Person of the Trinity, Jesus Christ.

What about the appearance of God in the Temple, portrayed to us in *Isaiah 6*?

- In the year that King Uzziah died, I saw the Lord seated on a throne, high and exalted, and the train of his robe filled the temple. (*Isaiah 6:1-2*)

Did Isaiah actually see God the Father? Not according to the Apostle John. He identifies the One Whom Isaiah saw as Jesus. In addition to the quotation from *Isaiah 6*, John quoted several other passages from Isaiah and then made this categorical statement:

- Isaiah said this because he saw Jesus' glory and spoke about him. (*John 12:41*)

Without an adequate understanding of the multiple Persons of the Godhead, there is no way to resolve some of these Scriptural paradoxes. And yet, when these and similar verses are properly understood, they provide us with wonderful glimpses of the Trinity in the Torah.

***

God gave Israel many previews, or foreshadowings, of the Cross. He was always preaching the Gospel. Shortly after celebrating God's goodness in bringing them to safety through the sea, the Israelites rebelled against the Lord. They were so thirsty that they wanted to kill Moses for bringing them out of Egypt. He cried out to the Lord.

- And the LORD said unto Moses, Go on before the people, and take with thee of the elders of Israel; and thy rod, wherewith thou smotest the river, take in thine hand, and go. Behold, I will stand before thee there upon the rock in Horeb; and thou shalt smite the rock, and there shall come water out of it, that the people may drink. And Moses did so in the sight of the elders of Israel. (*Exodus 17:5-6*, KJV)

Israel had wanted to indict God, and He was surprisingly ready to submit to their charges. Moses was instructed to take his staff of judgment and, followed by the elders, walk through the midst of the people. The Israelites would have unmistakably perceived that Moses' actions were a sign that there was about to be a trial and an execution. God would stand on the rock before them as a defendant, and Moses would symbolically strike Him down with his staff. However, instead of Israel being punished for their rebellion against God, God would suffer the very execution, which Israel deserved, while they would be blessed exceedingly from the most unlikely place. From a rock, life-giving waters would flow.

From the most unlikely place, this world would later be blessed. In the midst of the worst rebellion imaginable, Israel and the Gentiles would strike down the Savior of the world on a cross. However, instead of punishment for this most heinous of crimes falling upon the guilty, judgment would fall upon the innocent One. Those who were deserving of the ultimate chastisement would be blessed.

Are we wrongly reading this interpretation into the Torah? Is it really there? According to Paul, it is:

- ...and all [Israel] ate the same spiritual food, and all drank the same spiritual drink. For they drank from the spiritual Rock that followed them, and the Rock was Christ. (*1 Corinthians 10:3-4*)

★★★

Here is another Gospel message from the pages of the Old Testament. In this account, the Israelites had once again rebelled against the Lord. As a result, they were dying from poisonous snake bites.

- The LORD said to Moses, "Make a fiery serpent and set it on a pole, and everyone who is bitten, when he sees it, shall live." So Moses made a bronze serpent and set it on a pole. And if a serpent bit anyone, he would look at the bronze serpent and live. (*Numbers 21:8-9*)

Fifteen hundred years later, Jesus explained the symbolism:

- And as Moses lifted up the serpent in the wilderness, so must the Son of Man be lifted up, that whoever believes in him may have eternal life. (*John 3:14-15*)

Israel received physical healing by looking at an evil serpent that had been lifted up on a pole. We experience spiritual healing by looking to our Lord, who had been lifted up on the tree. Jesus had willingly taken evil upon Himself, becoming sin for us…"so that we might become the righteousness of God " (*2 Corinthians 5:21*).

✱✱✱

God sometimes uses the unlikeliest people to spread His Good News. For example, the Lord revealed King Jesus even to a false prophet, Balaam. God had given him a series of astounding prophecies. According to *Numbers 24:5*, Balaam was enabled to see the loveliness of Israel's tents—though they were worn out. Even more impressive, Balaam was shown an Israel without any iniquity:

- No misfortune is seen in Jacob,
  no misery observed in Israel.
  The LORD their God is with them;
  the shout of the King is among them.
  (*Numbers 23:21*)

How could this be? Their King was in their midst. His Presence made all the difference!

After this, God again revealed to Balaam this mysterious King in the midst of Israel. Paradoxically, Balaam prophesied:

- I see him, but not now; I behold him, but not near: a star shall come out of Jacob, and a scepter shall rise out of Israel. (*Numbers 24:17; see also Genesis 49:10*)

Israel's King was there, but He wasn't. He was present, but not in His fullness.

Much later (unwittingly) the Roman magistrate Pilate…

- …wrote an inscription and put it on the cross. It read, "Jesus of Nazareth, the King of the Jews." (*John 19:19*)

However, this title troubled the chief priests:

- So the chief priests of the Jews said to Pilate, "Do not write, 'The King of the Jews,' but rather, 'This man said, I am King of the Jews.'" Pilate answered, "What I have written I have written." (*John 19:21-22*)

It would stand. Interestingly, Jesus never called Himself "King of the Jews." Instead, Pilate had seemingly been divinely led to write this. One evil man (Balaam) had prophesied the coming King. Another evil man (Pilate) highlighted the partial fulfillment of this prophecy. And the rabbis could do nothing to change what had been destined.

***

Usually, when we think of Christ in the Pentateuch, we think of this prophecy of Moses:

- The LORD your God will raise up for you a prophet like me from among you, from your brothers—it is to him you shall listen… 'I will raise up for them a prophet like you from among their brothers. And I will put my words in his mouth, and he shall speak to them all that I command him. And whoever will not listen to my words

214

that he shall speak in my name, I myself will require it of him.' (*Deuteronomy 18:15, 18-19; see also Exodus 23:20-23*)

However, we must not overlook one last portrait of our Savior. Before the Israelites went in to the Promised Land, God gave Moses a song so that he could teach them about their future. Here are the last few lines:

- Rejoice, O nations, with his people, for he will avenge the blood of his servants; he will take vengeance on his enemies *and make atonement for his land and people*. (*Deuteronomy 32:43*, emphasis added)

How strange—God Himself would make atonement! What about the Levites, the priests? Why did He not appoint them to make atonement through the sacrificial system? The answer is profound: Only God could provide a truly adequate atonement. Only God could make a satisfactory payment for the sins of the world, a payment that the blood of animals would never be able to provide.

Jesus has mysteriously revealed Himself throughout the Pentateuch, all the books of Moses, the books of the Israelite nation, preaching His Good News to all who have the eyes to see and the ears to hear.

Without Jesus as the key, the Torah remains a shrouded mystery far removed from the understanding of the rabbis. Stumbling over Christ, they have had to resort to sensational means to make sense out of the Torah. Therefore, they often claim that the Torah cannot be literally understood. Consequently, they have invented other means to "understand" their Scriptures in a way that conforms to their traditions and have resorted to numerology, assigning numbers to each Hebrew letter. They then tally these numbers to derive meanings never intended by its Author. Meanwhile,

Moses instructed the Israelites that they didn't have to resort to extraordinary measures to understand and apply Scripture:

- For this commandment that I command you today is not too hard for you, neither is it far off. It is not in heaven, that you should say, 'Who will ascend to heaven for us and bring it to us, that we may hear it and do it?' Neither is it beyond the sea, that you should say, 'Who will go over the sea for us and bring it to us, that we may hear it and do it?' But the word is very near you. It is in your mouth and in your heart, so that you can do it. (*Deuteronomy 30:11-14*)

While Scripture is deep and rich, it is also plain and accessible to the unlearned. I hope that I have been able to make the reality of Christ in the Torah accessible for you. I also hope that I have been able to demonstrate the unity of the Bible. I have found that, when we are enabled to see this unity and singleness of God's plan, we will see the providential hand of God and be greatly encouraged in our faith.

***

JESUS IN THE BOOK OF JOSHUA

The clearest indication of Jesus in Joshua appears after Israel had crossed the Jordan River into the Promised Land and encamped on the Plains of Jericho, where they faced a great fortified city:

- When Joshua was by Jericho, he lifted up his eyes and looked, and behold, a man was standing before him with his drawn sword in his hand. And Joshua went to him and said to him, "Are you for us, or for our adversaries?" And he said, "No; but I am the commander of the army of the LORD. Now I have come." And Joshua fell on his face to the earth and worshiped and said to him, "What does my lord say to his servant?" And the commander of the LORD's army said to Joshua, "Take off your sandals from your feet, for the place where you are standing is holy." And Joshua did so. (*Joshua 5:13-15*)

Although this visitor is not identified as the "Angel of the Lord," as He often is in the Pentateuch, it is clear that He is divine:

1. Joshua worshipped Him, and He received this worship without objecting.
2. Joshua had been instructed to take off His sandals because the presence of God made this place holy.
3. The next two verses reveal that Joshua had been talking with Yahweh:

   o Now Jericho was shut up inside and outside because of the people of Israel. None went out, and none came in. And the LORD ["Yahweh"] said to Joshua, "See, I have given Jericho into your hand, with its king and mighty men of valor. (*Joshua 6:1-2*)

The "Commander of the LORD's army" is here referred to as "Yahweh." This indicates that He is both God and as the "Commander of the LORD's army," He is also distinct from "Yahweh." This gives us a glimpse of the NT doctrine of the Trinity, which we had been observing in the Pentateuch and will again observe in the next book of the Bible – Judges.

***

JESUS IN THE BOOK OF JUDGES

Evidence of Jesus is found throughout the Hebrew Scriptures. For now, I just want to focus on His appearances in *Judges*.

Why is it important to find these many appearances or indications of Jesus in the Hebrew Scriptures? It is one way to demonstrate the unity of the Bible. This unity points to the fact that it has one single superintending Author, the Holy Spirit. Well, why is this important? Because the Bible is often charged with being the work of man and not of God, despite the Bible's consistent insistence that it is fully God-breathed out! (*2 Timothy 3:16-17*)

Well, couldn't a series of editors have manufactured this unity? Theoretically, yes! However, the unity we find in the OT's testimony to Jesus is often so cryptic that editors would have ignored these perplexing indications or would have simply eliminated them.

In the *Book of Judges*, we encounter Jesus initially as the "Angel ("messenger" is an alternative translation from the Hebrew) of the Lord" ("Yahweh" in the Hebrew):

- Now the angel of the LORD went up from Gilgal to Bochim. And he said, 'I brought you up from Egypt and brought you into the land that I swore to give to your fathers. I said, 'I will never break my covenant with you, and you shall make no covenant with the inhabitants of this land; you shall break down their altars.' But you have not obeyed my voice. What is this you have done? So now I say, I will not drive them out before you...' (*Judges 2:1-3* ESV)

This Angel is no mere messenger. He claims far more about Himself:

1. That *HE* had brought Israel out of Egypt to the Promised Land
2. That the covenant was His, and
3. That Israel had failed to obey Him, as if He is God Himself.

Was He just God's mouthpiece uttering the words of God? The Angel's next appearance argues against this theory. Israel had been oppressed by their Midianite occupiers for years. The Angel of the Lord appeared to Gideon and told him that He would rid the land of the Midianites through this unlikely Israelite. To convince the skeptical Gideon, He performed a number of miraculous signs:

- Then Gideon perceived that he was the angel of the LORD. And Gideon said, 'Alas, O Lord GOD! For now I have seen the angel of the LORD face to face." But the LORD ["Yahweh"] said to him, "Peace be to you. Do not fear; you shall not die.' (*Judges 6:22-23*)

"Yahweh" is often used interchangeably with the "Angel of "Yahweh," suggesting that they are One although distinct. This phenomenon is even more clearly presented in the account of Moses' exchange with God, while He was shepherding the flock of his father-in-law:

- And the angel of the LORD appeared to him in a flame of fire out of the midst of a bush. He looked, and behold, the bush was burning, yet it was not consumed… God called to him out of the bush, "Moses, Moses!" And he said, "Here I am." Then he said, "Do not come near; take your sandals off your feet, for the place on which you are standing is holy ground." (*Exodus 3:2-5*)

This account claims that the "Angel" had been in the "midst of a bush. Then it claims the God was in the bush, indicating that both individuals are God. Moses was then required to remove his sandals because of the presence of *God* rather than a mere angel.

Similarly, when Gideon realized that he had been in the presence of the Angel of the Lord, he asked the "Lord God" if he was now going to die. "Yahweh" answered that he would not die. He didn't say, "You don't have to worry, since the Angel is not God. He's just a created being." Instead, He left Gideon with the impression that the Angel is God!

The last instance of the appearance of the Angel is even more dramatic. He appeared to the barren and unnamed wife of Manoah, to inform her that she would bear a son, Samson. Later, he appeared again to both of these future parents. Manoah then asked to know His identity. The Angel responded that he should have already perceived His true identity. He then ascended in a flame to erase any doubt. When Manoah saw this, he knew that they had been conversing with the Angel of the Lord who Manoah knew to also be God:

- And Manoah said to his wife, "We shall surely die, for we have seen God." But his wife said to him, "If the LORD had meant to kill us, he would not have accepted a burnt offering and a grain offering at our hands, or shown us all these things, or now announced to us such things as these." (*Judges 13:22-23*)

Manoah and his wife weren't the only ones who realized that God could appear in human form. Abraham must have understood this as he intervened with God on behalf of Lot (*Genesis 18*). Jacob certainly understood this after he had wrestled with the Angel and claimed that he had seen God face-to-face.(*Genesis 32; 48:15-16*)

They understood that the Angel was a distinct person from God but also God. The very fact that they identified Him as the "Angel of the Lord ['Yahweh'],'" also showed that they understood that there was a distinction between the two.

But was the Angel the second Person of the Trinity. Well, we know that God the Father dwells in unapproachable light and cannot be seen (*1 Timothy 6:16*). Could the Angel have been the Holy Spirit? This is highly unlikely. Instead, the Spirit is introduced immediately afterwards, and He plays a very different role:

- And the woman bore a son and called his name Samson. And the young man grew, and the LORD blessed him. And the Spirit of the LORD began to stir him in Mahaneh-dan, between Zorah and Eshtaol. (*Judges 13:24-25*)

Never do we see any Scriptural indication that the Spirit or the Father take on human form. This observation leaves us with Jesus alone.

Why is all of this important? It indicates that Scripture is a unified collection of documents spanning 1,500 years, three different languages, and across many different cultures. It reflects a single grand plan, which its human authors could not have concocted. It was also written, for the most part, by simple people, and not by learned rabbis, who were often martyred for what they had written. They never recanted but certified the truth of their message with their blood.

WORKS CITED

Pache, Rene, *The Return of Jesus Christ*, Translated by William Sanford LaSor, (Chicago: Moody Press, Eighth Printing, 1971)

Chapter 19

THE HIDDEN MESSIAH AND HIS COVENANT

What if we were to observe that the Old and New Testaments fit together like the functioning parts of a clock? Wouldn't it be fair to conclude that they must together represent one overarching plan and design? I think so and hope to provide one small glimpse of this design in this chapter.

Our Lord gave us a very peculiar revelation in *Psalm 25*:

- Who is the man who fears the LORD? Him will he instruct in the way that he should choose. His soul shall abide in well-being, and his offspring shall inherit the land. The friendship of the LORD is for those who fear him, and he makes known to them his covenant. (*Psalm 25:12-14*; ESV)

Here is what I had been pondering: Hadn't the Lord already revealed His covenant to Israel? Wasn't it at the center of the Hebrew Scriptures? Certainly! To what then was our Lord referring? Evidently, to the New Covenant – a Covenant found in cryptic ways in the shadows of the Old!

This seems to suggest that God hides certain truths, and He clearly does (*Proverbs 25:2; Deuteronomy 29:29; Isaiah 49:2*). It is not surprising that God's greatest secret was hidden away in the most holy place of the Temple, where only the high priest could enter and only once a year, on the Day of Atonement.

The "atonement cover," also translated as the "mercy seat" (KJV), covered the Ark of the Covenant, and was itself covered by the massive wings of two golden cherubim to prevent it from being seen. When the high priest entered this holiest place on that holiest day—Yom Kippur—he had to enter with great plumes of smoke generated by his incense censer, to prevent him from seeing the mercy seat and being struck dead (*Leviticus 16:2*):

- Aaron shall bring the bull for his own sin offering to make atonement for himself and his household, and he is to slaughter the bull for his own sin offering. He is to take a censer full of burning coals from the altar before the LORD and two handfuls of finely ground fragrant incense and take them behind the curtain. He is to put the incense on the fire before the Lord, and the smoke of the incense will conceal the atonement cover above the Testimony [the Ten Commandments which had been placed in the ark], so that he will not die. (*Leviticus 16:11–13*, NIV)

It wasn't just the smoke that had been designated to hide the "atonement cover." Two cherubim with spread wings were also positioned to hide this cover. This provokes many questions. Why should the atonement cover, or mercy seat, be so carefully concealed, and why with an accompanying threat of death? Shouldn't something called the "mercy seat" have been foremost among God's self-disclosures? Why wouldn't God want to display the fullness of His mercy to a people who needed it daily?

Seeing God could also bring death (*Exodus 33:20; Genesis 32:30; Judges 13:22*). Was this threat related to the danger of seeing the mercy seat? Adding to this mystery, the mercy seat rested above the ark containing the tablets of the Ten Commandments. This seems to suggest that this mysterious cover might even have had a greater stature than the Law.

God would meet with Israel above the mercy seat (*Exodus 30:6*), where He was mysteriously "enthroned between the covering cherubim" (*1 Samuel 4:4; 2 Samuel 6:2; Psalm 80:1; 99:1*). This mercy seat seemed to have been intimately related to God's provision of mercy. Why then would God so strenuously hide it?

The mercy seat was associated with the other divine mysteries: God's atonement, new covenant, and Messiah. Although He had ordained the Levites to make atonement for Israel's sins, He cryptically revealed that He would provide the decisive atonement: "Rejoice, O nations, with his people, for he will avenge the blood of his servants; he will take vengeance on his enemies and make atonement for his land and people." (*Deuteronomy 32:43; Psalm 65:3; 79:9*) However, He conspicuously didn't disclose the redemption or atonement price:

- For this is what the LORD says: 'You were sold for nothing, and without money you will be redeemed.' (*Isaiah 52:3*)

Redemption always costs. What then would the atonement for God's people cost? This disclosure is curiously opaque. This takes us back to the question of the nature of the atonement cover resting on the ark and the Law it contained. Why this complex of mysteries—the atonement, its price, and its agent? Wasn't the Law, with its sacrificial system, adequate? Evidently not! Seemingly, this sacrificial system would be superseded by a new but still hidden atonement or mercy, the Savior Jesus.

However, according to *Psalm 25*, this truth was hidden in plain sight from those who were not ready to see it and perhaps even despise what is closest to the heart of our Lord.

The Hebrew Scriptures are home to many mysteries, all pointing to the Savior and His Gospel. Jesus even affirmed that these Scriptures are about Him:

225

- You search the Scriptures because you think that in them you have eternal life; and it is they that bear witness about me, yet you refuse to come to me that you may have life. (*John 5:39-40*)

This assertion gives us a green-light to search out Christ in the Hebrew Scriptures. Let's proceed by focusing on one little phrase – "the arm of the Lord". Let's take one enticing example:

- Truth is lacking, and he who departs from evil makes himself a prey. The LORD saw it, and it displeased him that there was no justice. He saw that there was no man, and wondered that there was no one to intercede; then HIS OWN ARM brought him salvation, and his righteousness upheld him. (*Isaiah 59:15-16; Ezekiel 22:30*)

The Lord was distressed by the lack of truth and justice, but there was no one to intercede on behalf of His people. Therefore, *He* would have to intercede with Himself to bring salvation, and His arm would be the Intercessor. However, it doesn't make any sense for Him to intercede with Himself unless He is a plurality of Persons. Is this what our Lord intends to reveal to us?

In a very similar verse, He says:

- For the day of vengeance was in my heart, and my year of redemption had come. I looked, but there was no one to help; I was appalled, but there was no one to uphold; so MY OWN ARM brought me salvation, and my wrath upheld me. (*Isaiah 63:4-5*)

Is our Lord speaking of a distinct Person bringing salvation? We find a parallel scene in the *Book of Revelation*, which might shed some light on this question. In this vision, no one was found righteous to unlock God's scroll, allowing God's redemptive plan to go forward:

- Then I [John] saw in the right hand of him who was seated on the throne a scroll written within and on the back, sealed with seven seals. And I saw a mighty angel proclaiming with a loud voice, "Who is worthy to open the scroll and break its seals?" And no one in heaven or on earth or under the earth was able to open the scroll or to look into it, and I began to weep loudly because no one was found worthy to open the scroll or to look into it. And one of the elders said to me, "Weep no more; behold, the Lion of the tribe of Judah, the Root of David, has conquered, so that he can open the scroll and its seven seals." (*Revelation 5:1-5*)

Only the Lamb of God was found worthy. It seems that it is He who is this same arm of God, the one who "brought…salvation" for God (*Isaiah 63:5*). A few verses later, we read about "the Angel of His Presence" who had brought salvation. Could this be the same Person?

- In all their affliction he was afflicted, and the ANGEL OF HIS PRESENCE saved them; in his love and in his pity he redeemed them; he lifted them up and carried them all the days of old. (*Isaiah 63:9*)

If He had redeemed them, He had to pay a redemption price for them, the very thing that the Son had done for us. Who is this "Angel of His Presence" who had saved them from Egypt? Is this another reference to the "arm of the Lord?"

- The LORD said to Moses, "Depart; go up from here, you and the people whom you have brought up out of the land of Egypt, to the land of which I swore to Abraham, Isaac, and Jacob, saying, 'To your offspring

I will give it.' I will send an angel before you, and I will drive out the Canaanites, the Amorites, the Hittites, the Perizzites, the Hivites, and the Jebusites. Go up to a land flowing with milk and honey; but I will not go up among you, lest I consume you on the way, for you are a stiff-necked people…My PRESENCE will go with you, and I will give you rest." (*Exodus 33:1-3,14*)

The Angel, also referred to as "My Presence" as a distinct Person. He would lead Israel out of Egypt (*Numbers 20:16*), because God the Father could not remain in close proximity to Israel:

- Behold, I send an <u>angel</u> [or "messenger" in the Hebrew] before you to guard you on the way and to bring you to the place that I have prepared. Pay careful attention to him and obey his voice; do not rebel against him, for he will not pardon your transgression, for my name is in him. (*Exodus 23:20-21*)

All of this sounds suspiciously like the second Person of the Trinity. For one thing, God's name – His character and essence – is in this angel, signifying that He is God. As we continue to examine references to the "arm of the Lord," I think that this will become more apparent. The arm also seems to be a Person:

- Behold, the Lord GOD comes with might, and HIS ARM rules for him; behold, his reward is with him, and his recompense before him. He will tend his flock like a shepherd; he will gather the lambs in his arms; he will carry them in his bosom, and gently lead those that are with young. (*Isaiah 40:10-11*)

His Arm rules. He gathers, carries, and gently leads His flock. He is the Good Shepherd (*John 10*). Israel was even waiting for the Arm of the Lord, who brings salvation:

- My righteousness draws near, my salvation has gone out, and my arms will judge the peoples; the coastlands hope for me, and for MY ARM they wait. Lift up your eyes to the heavens, and look at the earth beneath; for the heavens vanish like smoke, the earth will wear out like a garment, and they who dwell in it will die in like manner; but my salvation will be forever, and my righteousness will never be dismayed… O ARM of the LORD; awake, as in days of old, the generations of long ago. Was it not you who cut Rahab in pieces, who pierced the dragon? (*Isaiah 51:5-6; 9*)

His Arm is again associated with His salvation, something that the entire world awaits and will see. For whom do they wait? For a literal arm? No, for their Savior:

- The LORD has bared HIS HOLY ARM before the eyes of all the nations, and all the ends of the earth shall see the salvation of our God. (*Isaiah 52:10*)

Not only will the world see the Arm of the Lord, He will also die for the sins of the world:

- Who has believed what he has heard from us? And to whom has the arm of the LORD been revealed?... He was despised and rejected by men… Surely he has borne our griefs and carried our sorrows; yet we esteemed him stricken, smitten by God, and afflicted. But he was pierced for our transgressions; he was crushed for our iniquities; upon him was the chastisement that brought us peace, and with his wounds we are healed. (*Isaiah 53:1-5*)

The Arm is the Son of God Himself, the Savior of the world. This should not surprise us. Jesus, Himself, said that the

Hebrew Scriptures are about Him, and this is just what we are finding.

Nor should it surprise us to find that the Prophets explicitly inform us that the Messiah was intentionally hidden:

- Listen to me, O coastlands, and give attention, you peoples from afar. The LORD called me from the womb, from the body of my mother he named my name. He made my mouth like a sharp sword; in the shadow of his hand he hid me; he made me a polished arrow; in his quiver he hid me away. (*Isaiah 49:1-2; 51:16*)

But why are these Scriptures so cryptic and the Messiah so hidden? Why not more explicit? For one thing, we can profitably handle only so much light. God discloses it to us in incremental digestible portions. Jesus declared that His disciples were not yet ready for full disclosure:

- I still have many things to say to you, but you cannot bear them now. (*John 16:12*)

For another thing, the world was not supposed to see what was intended for His Chosen. Jesus purposely taught in parables for this reason. He warned us to not throw our pearls of wisdom before swine (*Matthew 7:6*). However, the Father had other reasons to hide Jesus and His New Covenant:

- But we impart a secret and hidden wisdom of God, which God decreed before the ages for our glory. None of the rulers of this age understood this, for if they had, they would not have crucified the Lord of glory. (*1 Corinthians 2:7-8*)

But why would God hide the revelation of His mercy? I think that as the natural must precede the spiritual, so too must the law precede mercy. Why? Mercy is shallow, meaningless, and even contemptable unless we first have a deep understanding of our *need* for mercy – that we are sinners who deserve only death and damnation (*Romans 6:23*). The gift of life is not a gift as long as we think that we deserve it as our entitlement. The law illuminates our sin, showing us that we are only entitled to death. (*Romans 3:19-20; Deuteronomy 27:26*)

Without this understanding, God's mercy is foolishness (*1 Corinthians 2:14*). The way to God's mercy must therefore be carefully elucidated. The lessons of the law must first humble us, as the sinner who had entered the Temple to pray (*Luke 18:9-14*). Only then can it serve as a teacher to lead us to the hidden Messiah. (*Galatians 3:24*)

Could a multitude of human authors separated by 1500 years have invented such a hidden but yet integrated mosaic? Instead, such deep and internal harmony can only be the workings of One Grand Designer.

Chapter 20

CHRIST IN THE PSALMS

The Bible isn't two distinct Books – the Old and the New Testaments – but one integrated revelation of God. It couldn't be the product of men. Why not? The two Testaments together reflect an uncanny harmony which couldn't have been replicated by the multitude of Biblical authors if they had been writing without the inspiration and guidance of the Holy Spirit.

Nor is this unity a surface unity, one that could easily be manufactured by man in an attempt to prove that God is the ultimate author. Instead, it is a unity observed on a deep and cryptic level that defies human invention. The Psalms offer us a good example of this.

After Jesus' resurrection, He appeared to His fearful disciples who were hiding behind locked doors and declared that even the Psalms bore witness to Him and also had to be fulfilled:

- Then he said to them, "These are my words that I spoke to you while I was still with you, that everything written about me in the Law of Moses and the Prophets and the Psalms must be fulfilled." Then he opened their minds to understand the Scriptures. (*Luke 24:44-45*)

If our minds are opened to this reality, we can find great encouragement and one more reason to regard Scripture as the Word of God.

Usually, when we think of Messianic passages in the Psalms, which the New Testament identifies as fulfilled, these verses are likely to come to mind:

- Why do the nations rage and the peoples plot in vain? The kings of the earth set themselves, and the rulers take counsel together, against the LORD and against his Anointed [or "Messiah"]...I will tell of the decree: The LORD said to me [the Messiah], "You are my Son; today I have begotten you [from the dead]. Ask of me, and I will make the nations your heritage, and the ends of the earth your possession." (*Psalm 2:1-2, 7-8*; fulfilled according to *Acts 4:25-26; 13:33; Hebrews 1:5; 5:5*)

Jehovah's Witnesses wrongly claim that to be "begotten" *always* means to be birthed into existence. However, this passage will not allow them to do this. The Father informs His Son "Today I have begotten You." However, if He was just birthed into existence, the Father couldn't have said this to Him. Besides, the nations had been plotting against the Messiah even before He was begotten. Instead, the context argues that "begotten" is associated with being made the heir to everything that the Father owns.

Psalm 16 is another *Psalm* which the NT identifies as Messianic:

- Therefore my heart is glad, and my whole being rejoices; my flesh also dwells secure. For you will not abandon my [David's] soul to Sheol, or let your holy one [the Messiah] see corruption. You make known to me the path of life; in your presence there is fullness of joy; at your right hand are pleasures forevermore. (*Psalm 16:9-11; Acts 2:25-28, 31; 13:35*)

Both Peter and Paul cite this Psalm as a prophecy that the Christ will be raised from the dead, since His body will not decay as David's had.

Psalms 22, 40, and 69 picture the crucifixion:

233

- My God, my God, why have you forsaken me?...they divide my garments among them, and for my clothing they cast lots…I will tell of your name to my brothers; in the midst of the congregation I will praise you. (*Psalm 22:1, 18, 22; Matthew 27:35, 46; Mark 15:34; John 19:24*)

However, there are other portraits of Jesus, which I find far more impressive, although often overlooked. We sometimes find perplexing statements like the assertion that God didn't delight in animal sacrifices (*Psalm 51:16-17; 40:6*). This is strange because the entire sacrificial system demanded these sacrifices. It was through these required sacrifices that Israelites were reconciled to their God. Besides, the aroma of the offerings was described as pleasing to the Lord. (*Exodus 29:18, 25*)

This sounds like a contradiction. How is it possible that God was both pleased and not pleased by these offerings? The answer seems to be that He was not pleased by the offerings themselves. His creation had been one where there was no death, and His future kingdom would be one of complete peace where no pain or death will be found. Therefore, animal sacrifice is not His ideal. Nor should we expect that He would find this institution satisfying.

What then could be pleasing about the offering? Simply what it symbolized – the ultimate and future offering that would accomplish reconciliation:

- For it is impossible for the blood of bulls and goats to take away sins. Consequently, when Christ came into the world, he said, "Sacrifices and offerings you have not desired, but a body have you prepared for me; in burnt offerings and sin offerings you have taken no pleasure. Then I said, 'Behold, I [the Christ] have come to do your will, O God, as it is written of me in the scroll of the book.' (*Hebrews 10:4-7; quoting Psalm 40:5-7 in the LXX*)

All of the animal sacrifices had been pointing to the Christ. Once He accomplished His purpose, these sacrifices were no longer acceptable. They had merely served as preparation for the one Sacrifice that could reconcile humankind to God.

Christ is the key who brings harmony to the Scriptures. Without Him, we are left with a contradiction that God can be pleased and not be pleased simultaneously.

Here is another apparent contradiction that Christ resolves. Under the Mosaic Covenant, the Levites had been designated to perform the sacrifices that brought the mercy of God upon the people. However, *God* is identified as the Redeemer in many verses, especially in the Psalms. Why must God redeem or provide the atonement when He had designated the Levites to redeem?

- When iniquities prevail against me, you [God] atone for our transgressions. (*Psalm 65:3*)

What was the matter with the Mosaic sacrificial system that God would have to make the atonement? And what price would He be paying? This would remain a mystery until the Cross.

To add to this mystery, it seems that the Israelites were never able to make a sufficient offering for their sins.

- Truly no man can ransom another, or give to God the price of his life, for the ransom of their life is costly and can never suffice, that he should live on forever and never see the pit…But God will ransom [redeem] my soul from the power of Sheol, for he will receive me. (*Psalm 49:7-9, 15*)

235

This too is perplexing without reference to the Savior. Wouldn't animal sacrifices buy redemption? Evidently not! Why then the Mosaic system if it couldn't accomplish what it seemed to claim to accomplish? After all, even the Torah claimed that God would have to atone for the people:

- Rejoice, O nations, with His people; For He will avenge the blood of His servants, And will render vengeance on His adversaries, And will atone for His land and His people. (*Deuteronomy 32:43*; NASB)

Once again, Jesus is the key that unlocks and answers this paradox. No amount of animal sacrifices or Levites could atone for our sins or cleanse our conscience. Only the blood of Jesus (*Hebrews 9:13-15*), the atonement and redemption of God, could accomplish this.

Why then the Mosaic sacrificial system? It served as our schoolmaster that would led us to Jesus (*Galatians 3:22-24*).

We find Jesus in some Psalms, which seem to be entirely opposed to the Gospel, for example:

- LORD, who shall sojourn in your tent? Who shall dwell on your holy hill? He who walks blamelessly and does what is right and speaks truth in his heart; who does not slander with his tongue and does no evil to his neighbor, nor takes up a reproach against his friend; in whose eyes a vile person is despised, but who honors those who fear the LORD; who swears to his own hurt and does not change; who does not put out his money at interest and does not take a bribe against the innocent. He who does these things shall never be moved. (*Psalm 15:1-5*)

This Psalm totally depressed me. Why? Because it disqualified me from the possibility having a saving

236

relationship with the Lord. I wasn't blameless and I fell short of all the other requirements. Therefore, I had no confidence that such a God would receive me.

Later, I painfully encountered its sister *Psalm 24*:

- The earth is the LORD's and the fullness thereof, the world and those who dwell therein, for he has founded it upon the seas and established it upon the rivers. Who shall ascend the hill of the LORD? And who shall stand in his holy place? He who has clean hands and a pure heart, who does not lift up his soul to what is false and does not swear deceitfully. He will receive blessing from the LORD and righteousness from the God of his salvation... Lift up your heads, O gates! And be lifted up, O ancient doors, that the King of glory may come in. Who is this King of glory? The LORD ["Yahweh"], strong and mighty, the LORD, mighty in battle! Lift up your heads, O gates! And lift them up, O ancient doors, that the King of glory may come in. Who is this King of glory? The LORD of hosts, he is the King of glory! (*Psalm 24:1-10*)

This Psalm starts like *Psalm 15*, asking the question, "Who can dwell with the Lord," followed by demanding and depressing moral requirements. Once again, I realized that I lacked the necessary "clean hands and a pure heart." Struck out again!

However, I began to see that there is more here. The Psalm dramatically shifts at verse seven: "Lift up your heads, O gates...Oh ancient doors." It seemed as if the gates into the Temple, the place to find the mercy and forgiveness of God, were impassable. No one possessed the necessary entrance qualifications! However, there suddenly was the divine call to the gates to be lifted up! Why? There arrived another who did possess the necessary qualifications to pass through gate into the presence of God, "Yahweh" Himself!

Here is where it really got strange. Who is this person who had the qualifications to come before Yahweh? The King of glory! The Psalm answers this question twice to address the two earlier questions, "Who shall ascend… who shall stand in his holy place?" Again, the King of glory is the answer, but who is he? The Psalm answers, "The LORD ["Yahweh"] of hosts, he is the King of glory!"

What? Yahweh is coming into the presence of Yahweh? This must be a contradiction, right? Wrong! The Son of God is also God, Yahweh. He alone is worthy to come into the presence of His Father. The rest of us are utterly unworthy (*Luke 17:10*). We fall far short of the necessary qualifications.

How exhilarating! I no longer need to be perfect. Instead, my Savior is perfect, and He has gone into the presence of the Father on my behalf to liberate me from sin, guilt, and ultimately, my damnation.

In the *Book of Revelation*, the Apostle John was given a similar vision where no one was found worthy to come before the Lord to open the scroll. As the gates had been impassable because all were unworthy, John was shown that there was no possible way to proceed with the glorious plan of God, because no one was found worthy:

- Then I saw in the right hand of him who was seated on the throne a scroll written within and on the back, sealed with seven seals. And I saw a mighty angel proclaiming with a loud voice, "Who is worthy to open the scroll and break its seals?" And no one in heaven or on earth or under the earth was able to open the scroll or to look into it, and I began to weep loudly because no one was found worthy to open the scroll or to look into it. And one of the elders said to me, "Weep no more; behold, the Lion of the tribe of Judah, the Root of David, has conquered, so that he can open the scroll and its seven seals." (*Revelation 5:1-5*)

However, there was one piece of the equation that John was not seeing – the Lamb of God who is worthy to unlock the Father's plan. It is only through Him that the Gospel could go forth.

I now love these two Psalms. Why? They remind me of my hopeless condition and the Lamb of God who did for me what I couldn't do for myself.

How else can we understand these Psalms! The *Jewish Study Bible* blandly comments of *Psalm 15* that "This may be considered a Psalm of instruction, teaching the listener to become an individual who shall never be shaken." (p. 1297)

Fat chance! Instead, if we are honest with ourselves, without the "King of glory" coming on our behalf, we are relegated to one hopeless sobbing heap. What is the alternative? To live lives in the darkness of denial about our true status and condemned to always trying to prove our worthiness.

Here is what I love about these Psalms. I encounter the Savior of my soul in a hidden form but yet undeniably my Savior. I also see the one plan of God reaching its crescendo in the New Testament. We are privileged to be taken by the hand and led up to the top of the highest mountain where the blueprint contained in God's scrolls is unfolded for us.

WORKS CITED

The Jewish Study Bible, Jewish Publication Society, TANAKH Translation, Editors: Adele Berlin and Marc Zvi Brettler, (New York: Oxford University Press, 2004)

CONCLUSION

Matthew 24:35: *"Heaven and earth will pass away, but my words will not pass away."*

Upon the foundation, everything else stands. If the foundation moves, everything else is placed in jeopardy. So too with Scripture! If Scripture fails to provide a solid foundation for our lives, then our lives will be shaky and vulnerable to the slightest temptations or heresies. Jesus had likened this to building a house on the sand:

- Everyone then who hears these words of mine and does them will be like a wise man who built his house on the rock. And the rain fell, and the floods came, and the winds blew and beat on that house, but it did not fall, because it had been founded on the rock. And everyone who hears these words of mine and does not do them will be like a foolish man who built his house on the sand. And the rain fell, and the floods came, and the winds blew and beat against that house, and it fell, and great was the fall of it. (*Matthew 7:24-27*)

Jesus likened a sound foundation to building our lives on His teachings, the teachings of Scripture. When our homes are built on any other foundation, they will fall. Consequently, we have to build on this one foundation, as Paul had written:

- According to the grace of God given to me, like a skilled master builder I laid a foundation, and someone else is building upon it. Let each one take care how he builds upon it. For no one can lay a foundation other than that which is laid, which is Jesus Christ. (*1 Corinthians 3:10-11*)

However, we will not build on this one foundation unless we know that it is both secure and God-given. This is the reason for this book and for our need to know that this Bible is truly the Word of God.

I have merely scratched the surface of this rich and extensive subject. I hope that this book will motivate you to pursue this subject further.

www.ingramcontent.com/pod-product-compliance
Lightning Source LLC
LaVergne TN
LVHW051548080426
835510LV00020B/2913